ASIAPAC CULTURE

GATEWAY TO
CHINESE
CULTURE

Illustrated by Fu Chunjiang   **Translated by Y N Han and Geraldine Chay**

⚿ ASIAPAC • SINGAPORE

Publisher
ASIAPAC BOOKS PTE LTD
996 Bendemeer Road #06-09
Singapore 339944
Tel: (65) 6392 8455
Fax: (65) 6392 6455
Email: asiapacbooks@pacific.net.sg

Come visit us at our Internet home page
www.asiapacbooks.com

First published July 2003
10th print May 2010

© 2003 ASIAPAC BOOKS, SINGAPORE
ISBN 13   978-981-229-328-2
ISBN 10   981-229-328-0

Cover illustrations by Fu Chunjiang
Cover design by Joseph Tong
Body text in 11pt Times New Roman
Printed in Singapore by FuIsland Offset Printing (S) Pte Ltd

Publisher's Note

We are pleased to present Montage Culture, an exciting new series that takes the reader on a colourful journey to explore the history, origins, religions, customs and practices of various Asian groups.

The series has the theme of Many Faces, One World. Indeed, the events of recent times have affirmed that despite the diversities displayed among various people groups worldwide, our lives are interconnected, and the beliefs and actions of any one group do have a critical impact on the entire world, whether desirably or otherwise.

In this new era, the need for harmony is more pressing than ever. True harmony – local or universal – must only be achieved on the basis of mutual understanding and appreciation of other cultures besides one's own.

In publishing Montage Culture, we hope to play a part, albeit a small one, in promoting racial harmony in our country. The books are fully illustrated, making it easier for even young readers to enjoy the entire collection:

Montage Culture Series: Books entitled *Gateway to Peranakan | Malay | Indian | Chinese | Eurasian Culture.*
Montage Culture Packs: Delightful packs comprising books, posters, ethnic games, arts and crafts, and memorabilia such as *cherki* cards, five stones, Chinese chess, *bindhi* and bangles.

For *Gateway to Chinese Culture*, we would like to express our gratitude to Fu Chunjiang for the vivid illustrations, and the following for their unstinting support and assistance: the Singapore Federation of Chinese Clan Associations, Feng Ge, D' Art Station, Yong Gallery, Bao Yuan Trading Pte Ltd, S. I. Wood Carver and Chin Hing Emporium. Our thanks, too, to the production team for their best efforts in putting this book together.

About the Illustrator

Fu Chunjiang 傅春江 was born in Chongqing, China and received his BA in Chinese language and literature. A lover of Chinese culture, he is a versatile artist skilled in different styles, in particular the traditional style of comic books adapted from Chinese classics. His illustrations feature minute strokes, and clear and bright lines that can communicate the characters' rich and sincere feelings.

He has so far illustrated the following popular Asiapac titles: *Chinese Culture Pack*, *Origins of Chinese People and Customs*, *Origins of Chinese Culture*, *Gateway to Chinese Classical Literature*, *Essence of Traditional Chinese Medicine*, *Origins of Chinese Science and Technology*, *Origins of Chinese Festivals*, *Origins of Chinese Food Culture*, *Origins of Chinese Tea and Wine* and *Stories of Honour*.

Contents

Origins and History

Among the world's ancient civilisations, the Chinese nation is the only one that has not experienced any major cultural disruptions. Through more than 5,000 years of history, from the beginning of Chinese civilisation to the present, Chinese culture has been passed down despite many changes in government. Today, the Chinese people proudly call themselves descendants of Yan and Huang.

China's colourful culture is a result of its long history and geographical conditions. To the north of China is the Mongolian Plateau, to the west lie a desert and the Qinghai-Tibet Plateau, and to the east lies the sea. Such extraordinary natural boundaries have allowed Chinese culture to develop in relative isolation, resulting in its uniqueness.

A Look at the Chinese Nation

- China has a total population of more than 1.2 billion and is the world's most populous country.
- China is a unified and multi-ethnic country that is made up of 56 ethnic groups.
- Besides the majority Han ethnic group, there are numerous ethnic minorities, which together form 'the Chinese nation'.
- The Han ethnic group comprises 92 percent of the Chinese population.
- Among the ethnic minorities, the Zhuang has the largest population whereas the Hezhe and Luoba have the smallest.
- Although the population of the ethnic minorities is small, they inhabit a land area of 50 to 60 percent of China.
- Most of the ethnic minorities live in Yunnan Province. These include the Dai, Miao, Tibetan, Hui, Zhuang and Yao peoples.

China

The origins of China's name
Zhongguo, the Chinese name for China, first appeared in documents from the Zhou Dynasty (1100 BC – 221 BC), and was used in different senses in various historical periods.

It originally referred to the capital of the nation, where the emperor attended to state matters. In ancient times, the ruler often built his kingdom in the middle of the land, surrounded by vassal states big and small.

During the Spring and Autumn Period, the word was used to describe the vassal states near the lower reaches of the Yellow River (the Central Plains). This civilisation was more advanced and held itself apart from the barbarians around.

The people of the Han Dynasty named the empire they built from the Central Plains *Zhongguo* (Middle Kingdom). Later, the ethnic minority groups who conquered the land also used the name for their central governing body.

In ancient times, China was also called *Huaxia*. *Huaxia* meant a flourishing and glorious China. China can also be referred to as *Shenzhou* (the Divine Land), *Jiuzhou* (Nine Administrative Divisions) or *Zhongyuan* (Central Plains).

The Meaning of Chinese — *Hua*
The word *hua* as featured in *zhonghua* (Chinese) and *huaren* (the Chinese people) originally meant flower, but has gone on to signify civilisation, culture and literary grace. *Hua* also means beauty, goodness and splendour.

Hua in ancient inscriptions

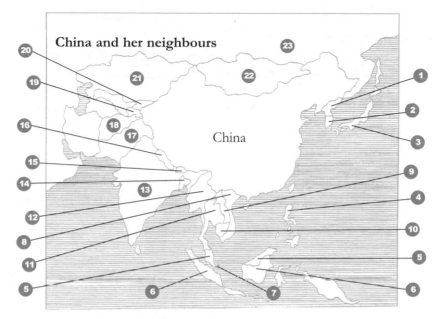

China and her neighbours

China

1. North Korea 2. South Korea 3. Japan 4. the Philippines 5. Malaysia 6. Indonesia
7. Singapore 8. Vietnam 9. Laos 10. Cambodia 11. Thailand 12. Myanmar 13. India
14. Bangladesh 15. Bhutan 16. Nepal 17. Pakistan 18. Afghanistan
19. Tadzhikistan 20. Kyrgyzstan 21. Kazakhstan 22. Mongolia 23. Russia

A Look at China's Geography

- China is located in east Asia and to the west of the Pacific Ocean. Its territory is often described as a golden rooster whose head faces the east with its tail to the west. Spanning a land area of 9.6 million square kilometres, China is almost as large as the whole of Europe.
- There are 14 countries that share borders with China.
  East – North Korea
  South – Myanmar, Laos, Vietnam
  West – Afghanistan, Pakistan
  Northwest – Kazakhstan, Kyrgyzstan, Tadzhikistan
  Southwest – India, Nepal, Bhutan
  North – Russia, Mongolia
- There are six nations across the sea: South Korea, Japan, the Philippines, Malaysia, Brunei and Indonesia.
- China has 34 provincial-level administrative areas, which include 23 provinces, five autonomous regions, four municipalities under the Central Government and two special administrative regions.

A mountainous land

China is a mountainous land, with higher elevations in the west. The mountainous regions amount to almost two-thirds of its entire land area.

China's Five Great Mountains are Mount Tai in the east, Mount Hua in the west, Mount Heng of Hunan in the south, Mount Heng of Shanxi in the north and Mount Song in the centre.

The Four Sacred Mountains of Buddhism are Mount Wutai in Shanxi, Mount Emei in Sichuan, Mount Jiuhua in Anhui and Mount Putuo in Zhejiang Province.

Huangshan in Anhui is famed throughout the world for its seas of mists, strange rock formations, oddly-shaped pine trees and hot springs.

Located in China's northwest are the Himalayas, as well as the Kunlun, Tanggula and Tianshan ranges. Many rivers in China spring from their snow-capped peaks.

China's Most
- Situated along the borders of Tibet, India and Nepal is the Himalayan range, home to Mount Everest, the highest mountain in the world.
- The Qinghai-Tibet Plateau is the highest in the world and is also known as 'The Roof of the World'.
- The Tarim Basin in Xinjiang is the largest basin in China, in terms of area.
- The Taklimakan Desert is the largest desert in China.
- The Northeast Plain is the largest of the plains in China.
- Located in Qinghai Province, Qinghai Lake is the largest inland saltwater lake in China.
- The Grand Canyon of the Yarlung Zangbo River is the largest canyon in the world.

Beautiful Scenery

The Yellow River begins in the Bayankala Mountain Range in Qinghai Province and is China's second longest river, spanning a total of 5,464 kilometres as it meanders through nine provinces. Its basin was one of the earliest birthplaces of the Huaxia people and it is esteemed as the Mother River of the Chinese nation. It has also been a political, economic and cultural hub since ancient times — even Huangdi, ancestor of the Chinese people, numbers among those who made their home here. The capital cities of many dynasties were also located along the river. Examples are Chang-an (Xi-an), Luoyang, Xianyang, Kaifeng and Anyang. Many artefacts and traces of Old Stone Age and New Stone Age settlement have been found here, including the Lantian County in Shaanxi (home to the primitive man) and Banpo Village in Xi-an.

Dayu Harnesses the River
The mighty Yellow River often breaks its banks, causing massive floods. Dayu, the great hero who harnessed the river, used the diversion method to redirect the floodwaters to the  sea. While he was carrying out this task, he passed his home thrice but did not go in. After 13 years of hard work, the mammoth project was finally completed. Shun, the emperor then, gave up his throne to Dayu.

The Yangtze River rises from the Tanggula Mountain Chain in Qinghai Province. China's longest river, it has a length of 6,300 kilometres and passes through 11 provinces, autonomous regions and municipalities. It is also one of the earliest cradles of the Chinese nation. Many Old Stone Age and New Stone Age archaeological sites have been discovered here, including those of the Yuanmo Man and the Hemudu Culture. After the Tang Dynasty, the status of the Yellow River basin as a cultural and economic centre declined as a result of various factors, including wars, excessive cultivation and deforestation, and its cold and dry climate. China's economic and cultural activities gradually moved southwards to the Yangtze River region, which became the hub for supply of food, cotton and silk textiles and tax grants. The hydroelectric facility that is being built at the Three Gorges of Yangtze River will be the world's largest dam and power generator.

Ancient Humans in China

Yuanmou Man
The fossilised teeth of a Chinese primitive man were discovered by archaeologists in the county of Yuanmou in Yunnan Province. The bones date back to 1.7 million years ago. This is the oldest fossil discovered of the Chinese primitive man.

Lantian Man
The fossils of the Lantian Man were discovered in the county of Lantian in Shaanxi Province. It is 700,000 years old.

Peking Man
The fossils of the Peking Man were discovered on the outskirts of Beijing, in Zhoukoudian. His skull is about 500,000 years old.

Upper Cave Man
The Upper Cave Men lived in Longgu Hill, Zhoukoudian, Beijing. These people knew how to use fire and also produced the first bone needle used to sew animal hide. They lived almost 18,000 years ago.

The Neolithic Age

Originating from the middle reaches of the Yellow River, the Yangshao culture (5000 BC – 3000 BC) is the representative of the Neolithic Age. The culture is characterised by red pottery of fine clay and coloured pottery. The painted pottery of the Banpo culture of Xi'an in Shaanxi is most exquisite with its many decorative patterns, and is the finest of ancient art.

The Hemudu culture of Yuyao City, Zhejiang Province in the Yangtze River basin has its origins as early as the Yangshao culture. They had already learnt how to cultivate rice and build wooden houses with large wooden poles.

In the later part of the Neolithic Age, the art of pottery reached its zenith when the Longshan culture (2500 BC – 2000 BC) in Shandong managed to produce black pottery with sides as thin as eggshells!

The Three August Ones and the Five Lords

The Three August Ones and the Five Lords were the eight legendary wise rulers who had made great contributions to the Chinese culture.

The Three August Ones were namely Shennong, who developed agriculture; Suiren, who discovered fire; and Fu Xi, who developed pastoral farming, while the Five Lords were namely Huangdi, Zhuanxu, Di Ku, Yao and Shun. They were the five earliest emperors who built China.

Descendants of Yan and Huang – Yandi and Huangdi

In the distant past, the tribes sometimes came into conflict with each other. Huangdi and Yandi were leaders of two major tribes.

Yandi: Also known as Shennong, he was the leader of a western tribe. He was the first person to develop agriculture in China and increased the people's knowledge about herbal medicine.

Huangdi: Also known as Xuan Yuanshi, he was born around Shaanxi. Not only was he an inventor and legislator, his wife, Leizu, reared silkworms for silk to make clothes with. His subordinate, Cangjie, created Chinese characters.

At that time, there was a tribe in China's east named Chiyou. While advancing towards the central plains, the tribe clashed with Yandi. Yandi sought Huangdi's help and the two tribes fought off Chiyou. This was the famous Zhuo Lu Battle.

Later on, Yandi and Huangdi clashed and fought three battles at Banquan. Yandi was defeated and Huangdi became the chief of the alliance of tribes around the middle and lower reaches of the Yellow River. The Yan and Huang tribes merged to become the Huaxia (the origins of the Chinese nation).

As Yandi and Huangdi were the founders of the Chinese nation, the Chinese people often refer to themselves as descendants of Yan and Huang.

Fuxi: Fuxi had the head of a man and the body of a snake. He was both sibling and spouse to Nuwa. He created the famous Eight Trigrams and taught Man how to fish and domesticate animals.

Suiren: Suiren taught Man to make fire. This allowed Man to cook food and keep warm.

Zhuanxu: Grandson of Huangdi, he was an adept administrator and brought law and order to society.

Di Ku: Great-grandson of Huangdi, he followed the system of government set up by Huangdi and Zhuanxu, and the country prospered under his leadership.

The Story of Yao and Shun

I am old. I should look for a capable successor.

Your son Danzhu can take over from you.

Emperor Yao

Though he is my son, I want to find someone who has virtue and ability.

Shun was a poor commoner who had lost his mother when he was young. Though his father and stepmother ill-treated him, he remained filial.

Please eat, Father.

Shun developed a piece of wasteland at the foot of Mount Li and created pottery. Under the influence of Shun, the people at Mount Li stopped fighting among themselves and became gentlemen.

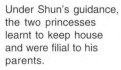

I shall marry my two daughters to you.

Under Shun's guidance, the two princesses learnt to keep house and were filial to his parents.

Yao then invited Shun to be regent and he brought peace and stability to the nation. Yao let Shun become emperor and was the first ruler to abdicate his throne to someone more capable.

Xia Dynasty — The first dynasty

Shun named as his heir Dayu, a hero who had managed to control the floods afflicting the people. After Dayu's death, his son ascended the throne, establishing the hereditary system and thus founding China's first dynasty.

Dayu's Nine Tripod Vessels

According to legend, after Dayu ascended the throne, he divided the country into nine administrative regions or states, represented by nine tripod vessels. These nine vessels signified *tianxia* (the land under heaven) and *wangquan* (state power). Later, people used the term *wending* (ask about the size and weight of the tripods) to mean an attempt to seize state power.

Shang Dynasty

The last Xia king Jie was the first infamous tyrant in China's history. Tang, the leader of the Shang tribe in the east, overthrew him and set up the Shang Dynasty.

Pan Geng, Shang's 20th ruler, moved the capital to Yin (now Xiaotun Village, Anyang County, Henan Province). Hence the Shang Dynasty is also known as Yin Dynasty or Shangyin.

Zhou Dynasty

Like Xia, the Shang Dynasty was ruined at the hands of another despot, King Zhou. Ji Chang (later known as King Wen of Zhou), was the leader of the Zhou tribe to the west. With the aid of Jiang Ziya (also known as Jiang Taigong or Taigongwang), Ji Chang strengthened his tribe. Ji Chang's son Ji Fa (later known as King Wu of Zhou) succeeded him after his death and led an alliance of tribes against Shang in what is now known as the Muye Battle. With Shang overthrown, the Zhou Dynasty was established. Many small states such as Lu, Qi, Wei and Jin, were formed and their rulers were called dukes or lords.

Duke Zhou (Zhou Gong)

Duke Zhou was the younger brother of King Wu of Zhou. After King Wu's death, Duke Zhou became the regent, assisting his nephew who became king. He helped lead the country to prosperity and established many rites and regulations.

The Spring and Autumn and Warring States Periods

China's third dynasty – the Zhou Dynasty – was split into Western and Eastern Zhou, with the latter also known as the Warring States of the Spring and Autumn Period. At that time, the king of Zhou had no real power and many smaller states seized the opportunity to wrangle for power. There were more than 100 vassal states when the Five Overlords of the Spring and Autumn Period appeared. They were Lord Huan of Qi, Lord Wen of Jin, Lord Mu of Qin, Lord Xiang of Song and King Zhuang of Chu. Most of the smaller kingdoms were assimilated by the more powerful ones during this time. Among them, the seven strongest – Qi, Chu, Yan, Han, Zhao, Wei and Qin – were known as the Seven Powers.

Many divergent schools of thought arose during this time, with the emergence of famous thinkers like Confucius, Mencius, Laozi, Zhuangzi and Sunzi.

To sleep on firewood and taste bile
(*wo xin chang dan* 卧新尝胆)

During the final years of the Spring and Autumn Period, the states of Wu and Yue were at war. King Helu of Wu died of battle wounds and his son Fuchai later won the battle against Yue.

The vengeful King Goujian of Yue slept on firewood and tasted bile each day to remind himself of his humiliation. After 10 years of preparation and strategising, he finally defeated King Fuchai and became the last overlord of this period.

Emperor Qin — China's first emperor

Qin Shihuang (Emperor Qin) conquered the warlords and unified China in 221 BC, ending the chaotic Spring and Autumn and Warring States Periods. Feeling that his achievement was glorious and unprecedented, Qin Shihuang combined the characters from the Three August Ones (*San Huang*) and the Five Lords (*Wu Di*) to coin the title of emperor (*huang di*).

As the first emperor, he also called himself Qin Shihuang. During his reign, Qin Shihuang unified the Chinese characters, currency, units of measurement, etc. However, he also earned a reputation as a tyrant by burying Confucian scholars alive, burning books and exploiting the people's wealth and labour to rebuild A-fang palace and his mausoleum on Mount Li.

望感石曆

Emperor Qin decided to adopt *Xiao Zhuan* (cursive script) as the uniform script for the whole country.

The 'half *liang*' round coin with the square hole in the middle was the only currency in the country.

The Great Wall of China

To prevent attacks from the northern nomadic tribes, Yan, Zhao and Qin had already begun building walls during the Spring and Autumn Period. After Emperor Qin unified the nation, he ordered the three walls to be linked up and extended. The Great Wall continued to be worked on until the Ming Dynasty. Emperor Kangxi stopped the work during the Qing Dynasty, saying, "It is not a wall of bricks I want but a wall of aspirations."

Fall of the Qin Dynasty

The Qin Dynasty lasted only 15 years. After the death of Qin Shihuang, his successor, Qin the Second, indulged in merry-making and left Zhao Gao to handle affairs of state. The tyranny of the two Qin emperors aroused much resentment among the people, and in 209 BC, Chen Sheng and Wu Guang led a peasant uprising against the Qin Dynasty. Though they were killed in the attempt, the flames of revolution they ignited spread and finally toppled the Qinynasty.

Raise the Standard of Revolt

In the twilight years of the Qin Dynasty, there was an ambitious man named Chen Sheng.

I am young and strong. I must achieve something huge next time!

We are just lowly peasants. Who are we to talk about career and riches!

Sigh! How would mere sparrows understand the lofty ideals of a swan?

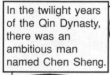

While they were at Dayi Village, it rained for several days and the troop was forced to stop, delaying their journey to Yuyang.

In AD 209, the Yangcheng provincial governor sent two military officers to escort 900 peasants to Yuyang to serve as sentry guards. Chen Sheng was one of them. He met Wu Guang on the way and the two became good friends.

If we miss the deadline, we'll be executed . Why not revolt? Better to die than to be killed!

All right! But we must do this to get everyone's support...

A piece of cloth with the words 'King Chen Sheng' was found in the stomach of a fish. A fox was heard crying, "Chu rejoices, King Chen Sheng!" Everyone started to discuss these incidents.

Wu Guang and Chen Sheng then killed the two officers escorting them.

A real man must not die for nothing!

Is a person's rank decided only by fate?

Everyone supported the movement. They made spears and flagpoles. This was China's first ever peasant uprising, called 'raising the standard of revolt'.

The first peasant emperor — Han Gaozu

Liu Bang, the founder of the Han Dynasty, was born into a poor peasant family. He overthrew the Qin emperor and became known as Han Gaozu (the ancestor of the Han people).

His greatest rival was Xiang Yu, the Tyrant of Chu. The two of them engaged in the famous Chu-Han War. In the end, with the assistance of talented men like Zhang Liang, Xiao He and Han Xin, Liu Bang drove Xiang Yu into a corner. It was at the River Wu that Xiang Yu killed himself with his own sword.

Peace and prosperity during the reign of Emperors Wen and Jing

After the demise of Emperor Gaozu of Han, Emperors Wen and Jing implemented the style of government and policy known as *xiuyang shengxi* (recuperation and regeneration). As a result, China prospered and the treasury was rich. This period was known as the Prosperous Age of Emperors Wen and Jing.

Emperor Wu of Han

Emperor Wu of the Han Dynasty expanded the western region and brought Western Han into a golden age. In history, he is often mentioned together with Emperor Qin Shihuang for their great achievements. Emperor Wu was a follower of Confucian teachings and used them when governing his nation.

Wang Mang usurps Han; prosperity of Guangwu

In 8 AD, Wang Mang stole power from the Han Dynasty and changed the title of the dynasty to Xin. In 25 AD, Liu Xiu, a descendant of Liu Bang, retrieved the throne and named himself Emperor Guangwu of Han. This period was called Eastern Han while the period before that was known as Western Han.

> #### Han Dynasty — the Han people
> The Han Dynasty lasted for more than 400 years, making it China's longest dynasty since its unification. It was also the powerful state in East Asia at the time. The people of the Han Dynasty became known as the Han people. After the demise of the Han Dynasty, the Han people continued to be termed the Hans.

Han Dynasty

Special powers of the Ministers and Imperial Maternal Relatives
In 88 AD, 10-year-old Emperor Hedi ascended the throne with Empress
Dowager Dou as regent. Emperor Hedi was followed by many other child
emperors and regent mothers, who sought support from their families by granting
them special powers. After the emperor grew up, he would empower the ministers
to get rid of his relatives. Once the emperor died, the relatives would install
another child emperor and begin another round of politicking, taking the Eastern
Han Dynasty on a gradual spiral of decline.

The Destruction of Factions
Towards the end of the Eastern Han Dynasty, intellectuals and imperial scholars
penned criticisms against the ministers who held extreme authority. The ministers
accused the intellectuals of forming traitorous factions and organised two
roundups of such faction members called 'the destruction of factions' during the
reign of Emperors Huandi and Lingdi. Many intellectuals and scholars were
arrested and thrown into prison. Some were imprisoned their whole lives.

The Yellow Turbans Uprising
In 184 AD, Zhang Jiao, leader of the Taiping Way, organised a nationwide uprising
with more than 300,000 followers. He propagated a slogan predicting the end of
the grey sky, and the emergence of the yellow sky in the year of *jia zi* (i.e., the
7th year of Emperor Lingdi's reign), which would be followed by great prosperity.
During the uprising, the soldiers wore yellow kerchiefs on their heads and were
dubbed Yellow Turbans. They burnt down feudal offices, confiscated the land
and property of landowners and opened the central food depository to help the
poor people. Thus, the Yellow Turbans were loved and grew in great numbers.

The Dong Zhuo Autocracy
The Eastern Han administration used provincial forces to quell the Yellow Turbans.
After Emperor Shaodi ascended the throne, Empress Dowager He's brother
He Jin became the regent. To diminish the power of the other ministers, he
summoned Dong Zhuo, a prefectural governor, to Beijing. After Dong Zhuo's
arrival, Emperor Shaodi was removed and Emperor Xiandi was installed. Dong
Zhuo appointed himself prime minister and held court. Other prefectures
denounced his autocratic actions and the nation disintegrated into various
territories. By then, Eastern Han was but a dynasty in name only.

The Three Kingdoms — the most well-known era

The famous Chinese classic novel, *Romance of the Three Kingdoms*, recounts the twilight years of the Han Dynasty, when years of incessant wars brought forth many men of talent who vied among themselves to rule the country. The most powerful were Cao Cao, Liu Bei and Sun Quan, who established the Wei, Shu (also known as Shu Han) and Wu States respectively. Wei was the biggest state while Shu was the smallest.

Cao Cao (Wei)   Liu Bei (Shu)   Sun Quan (Wu)

The Northern and Southern Dynasties — Wei and Jin

Shu was the first to fall. Two years later, Sima Yan took over Wei and conquered Wu to reunify China, founding the Jin Dynasty to become Emperor Wu of Jin.

The Jin Dynasty was divided into Eastern and Western Jin. Western Jin was destroyed by the northern Xiongnu tribe and the Sima family rebuilt Eastern Jin in Jiangnan. The northern tribes proclaimed themselves emperors of the northern plains, carving the land into more than 20 minor kingdoms known as Five *Hu** 16 Kingdoms. Following Eastern Jin's decline, the Jiangnan area was ruled by governments such as Song, Qi, Liang and Chen, and were collectively known as the Southern Dynasties. Emperor Daowu of Northern Wei managed to unify the north. In history, Northern Wei, Eastern Wei, Northern Qi, Western Wei and Northern Zhou were collectively known as the Northern Dynasties.

Sui Dynasty

The Sui Dynasty was established in 581 AD after Emperor Wen of Sui reunified China. After his death, his ambitious son, Yang Guang, engaged in countless wars, causing massive chaos. The Sui Dynasty thus ended very quickly.

> The Sui Dynasty first established the *keju* system (imperial examination for the selection of officials), which lasted for almost 1,000 years up till the end of the Qing Dynasty. Emperor Yang of the Sui Dynasty ordered the digging of the Grand Canal, which ran over 1,700 kilometres from Beijing to Hangzhou. The Grand Canal is the world's longest man-made waterway.

*In ancient times, the non-Han peoples were called Hu.

The Battle of Red Cliff

In 208 AD, the 50,000-strong combined forces of Sun Quan and Liu Bei squared off against the 800,000-strong army of Cao Cao at Red Cliff near the mouth of the Yangtze River.

Cao Cao's army far outnumbers ours, but they are bound to be weak because they have rushed here from afar. Their numbers won't matter.

Zhou Yu, Commander of the combined forces.

As Zhou Yu had predicted, the Cao army fell sick en masse and were defeated quickly.

As the Cao army was from the north, they were unused to the turbulent waters and chained their ships together.

The Cao army has lined up their vessels. We can use fire to attack.

Huang Gai, Zhou Yu's subordinate.

Pretending to surrender, Huang Gai led soldiers in 10 large boats towards the Cao armada.

They started a fire and charged into the midst of the Cao ships. As the Cao vessels were chained together, the fire spread quickly and the Cao army was defeated.

This dramatic victory became known as the Battle of Red Cliff. The ensuing stalemate between the kingdoms of Cao Cao, Sun Quan and Liu Bei is known in history as the Three Kingdoms Period.

Tang Dynasty — the most powerful and prosperous dynasty

Lasting 290 years, the Tang Dynasty was considered a golden age in the history of China, when its territories were vast and the arts flourished. Due to the great influence the dynasty wielded, foreigners called the Chinese people the 'Tang people' and Chinese dress the 'Tang costume'. Chinatown, where Chinese overseas congregate, became known as *Tangrenjie* (the Tang people's street).

Tang Taizong — the reign of Zhenguan

Tang Taizong, born Li Shimin, was the second emperor of the Tang Dynasty. He is also the most famous emperor in Chinese history. During his 23-year reign, the Tang Dynasty prospered. He conquered the northern and western regions and was hailed as the Khan of Heaven by the peoples of those regions. He was also a wise politician who recognised and appreciated abilities. He knew how to use people according to their abilities. He had compassion for his people. The country enjoyed stability both internally and externally. As the year of Tang Taizong was known as Zhenguan, history annals recorded his reign as the reign of Zhenguan.

The Three Mirrors of Emperor Taizong

Emperor Taizong once said, "Look into a copper mirror and you will check your dress and hat; use antiquity as a mirror and you will know the ups and downs of an empire; with people as a mirror, you will know right from wrong."

After Wei Zheng's death, Emperor Taizong felt as if he had lost a mirror.

Wu Zetian — China's only female emperor

Wu Zetian, Tang Gaozong's empress, removed the heirs to Tang Gaozong's throne and ascended the throne herself, renaming the dynasty the Zhou Dynasty. While merciless to those who opposed her, she was also able to recognise and use men of talent during her reign.

The prosperous years of Kaiyuan

The early years of Emperor Xuanzong's reign was China's most prosperous period, named *kaiyuan shengshi* (prosperous years of Kaiyuan). Chang'an, the capital, had a population of millions, and numerous foreign scholars, businessmen and ambassadors. Later, Emperor Xuanzong spent most of his attention on his beloved concubine Yang Guifei, resulting in the Insurrection of An Lushan and Shi Siming, and ultimately the fall of the Tang empire.

Zhu Wen seizes Tang

Huang Chao staged an uprising and conquered Chang'an in 881 AD. He proclaimed himself emperor, naming the new empire Great Qi. Later, Huang Chao's subordinate, Zhu Wen, defected to the Tang forces, diminishing his strength. Huang Chao was defeated and killed in 884 AD. Though the uprising was quelled, it had seriously shaken the Tang administration.

The Tang emperor bestowed the name 'Quanzhong' (all loyalty) on Zhu Wen. However, Zhu Wen usurped the throne in 907 AD and established the short-lived Liang Dynasty, ending the almost 300-year-old Tang Dynasty.

The Rebellion of An Lushan and Shi Siming

To strengthen the defence of the empire, Emperor Tang Xuanzong built 10 regional commanderies at the borders.

An Lushan, a regional commander of non-Han descent at Pinglu Station, searched everywhere for rare and unique animals and treasures to amuse Emperor Xuanzong. Thus, the emperor and his beloved concubine Yang Guifei (Concubine Yang) liked him a lot.

What is in this huge stomach of yours?

It's the most sincere heart.

The son pays his respects to his mother!

How funny! Why don't you be my godson?

Not knowing what An Lushan had up his sleeve, Emperor Xuanzong and Concubine Yang were delighted.

An Lushan secretly built up an army. In 755 AD, he led more than 10,000 soldiers and horses into the capital in an attempt to usurp the throne.

It's all because the emperor let Concubine Yang's brother Yang Guozhong be prime minister!

Emperor Xuanzong escaped with his beloved concubine and came to Mawei Hill. Agitated and exhausted, his guards killed Yang Guozhong and demanded Concubine Yang's life as well.

Emperor Xuanzong had no choice but to sentence Concubine Yang to death. Lasting eight years, the rebellion broke the Tang Dynasty's image of prosperity and the Tang Dynasty went into decline.

Draping the yellow robe — the establishment of the Song Dynasty

In 960 AD, General Zhou Kuangyin of Later Zhou led a rebellion at Chenqiao. His soldiers draped a yellow robe over him and declared him emperor. Zhao Kuangyin thus became Emperor Taizu of the Song Dynasty. To consolidate his rule and centralise control, he threw a banquet for his generals where he took back military power. This would later be called 'taking back power with a cup of wine'.

Incursions from the north

During the Northern Song Dynasty, the kingdoms of Liao and Xixia in the north gradually grew in strength and made several incursions into the Central Plains. In order to put an end to these disturbances, the Song empire signed peace agreements with the Liao and Xixia kingdoms, promising heavy annual tributes of silver and silk. Song even became brotherly with Liao and called the Liao empress dowager aunt.

Wang Anshi Reform

Due to the endless internal disturbances and foreign aggression, the imperial coffers were rapidly depleted by attempts to strengthen the army and pay the tributes. This resulted in the decline of the Song Dynasty. During the reign of Emperor Shenzong, the emperor attempted to restructure the government and appointed Wang Anshi Prime Minister, tasking him with the reform of the finance and military divisions. This was known as the Wang Anshi Reform. The reform ended in less than 10 years due to the strong opposition of Sima Guang and others.

Sima Guang
Sima Guang was a famous historian who wrote *Zi Zhi Tong Jian* (*Comprehensive Mirror for Aid in Government*), a chronicle covering over 1,300 years of history.

Crisis of Jingkang

In the northeast, the Nüzhen tribe set up the Kingdom of Jin which destroyed Liao with its strong forces and ravenously eyed the land on which the Song empire stood. In 1127, the Song Dynasty was shaky with Song Weizong and Qinzong taken prisoner by the Jins.

When Song Gaozong ascended the throne, he had the capital moved from Kaifeng to Lingan. From then on, that era became known as the Southern Song Dynasty and the former dynasty became the Northern Song Dynasty.

Yue Fei — China's most famous general

Yue Fei is China's best known general. He had won several engagements against the invading Jin army. But Premier Qin Hui initiated negotiation talks with the Jins. He incited Song Gaozong to recall Yue Fei from the battlefied and framed Yue Fei. The latter was imprisoned and executed as a result.

The peace treaty between Song and Jin

To maintain stability, the Southern Song administration decided to sue for peace with the Jin kingdom. In their first treaty in 1142, the Jin people embraced the Song emperor as their ruler and they were the ministers. However, Song had to give 250,000 taels of silver and 250,000 bolts of silk to Jin yearly. Later, after Song failed in two punitive expeditions against Jin, they were forced into a second negotiation where Song was to call Jin 'younger uncle'. In their third negotiation, Song was made to call Jin 'elder uncle'. At this point, the Southern Song Dynasty had no way of returning to its days of prosperity.

Wen Tianxiang

Meanwhile, the Mongols became extremely powerful. In 1271, they invaded Southern Song. Wen Tianxiang organised an army to repel the Mongol army, but was defeated. Refusing to surrender, he wrote patriotic poems such as 'Zheng Qi Ge' (Song of Justice) and 'Guo Ling Ding Yang' (Sailing on a Lonely Ocean). Pressed by Mongol forces, the Song Prime Minister Lu Xiufu jumped into the sea with the child emperor and drowned in 1279, bringing the Southern Song Dynasty to a close.

Genghis Khan — the Emperor of the universe

The Mongolians once established an empire in the 13th century that went beyond Asia to Europe. It was an unprecedented achievement in the history of China. This empire was ruled by its founder Genghis Khan and his descendants. Genghis Khan, who was born Tiemuzhen, became hailed as the Great Khan and Genghis Khan after he unified the northern tribes, meaning 'the emperor of the universe'. After establishing the empire of Mongolia, Genghis Khan turned his attention to conquering other lands. Within a few decades, the Mongolian forces had seized many cities and moats. At its height, it extended over most of Asia — the largest land empire in history.

The founding of the Yuan Dynasty

Kublai Khan, the son of Genghis Khan, became Mongolia's fifth Khan. His troops attacked Southern Song and established the Yuan Dynasty. He became known as the ancestor of the Yuans — Yuan Shizu. The territory occupied by the Yuan Dynasty was larger than any other dynasty recorded in the history of China. Many Europeans, including the famous Italian traveller Marco Polo, visited China at that time, greatly boosting the cultural exchange between the East and the West.

Marco Polo

The famous Italian explorer Marco Polo came to China during the Yuan Dynasty and stayed for 17 years. Kublai Khan greatly admired Marco Polo and even conferred on him a government post which enabled him to travel freely within China. In his book *Travels of Marco Polo*, he vividly described China, which greatly stirred the Europeans' interest in the Far East.

Genghis Khan

Tiemuzhen, better known as Genghis Khan, was the son of Yesugai, leader of the Qiyan tribe in Mongolia.

When Tiemuzhen was nine, Yesugai was murdered by another tribe.

One day, I shall be the great hero of the steppes and those tribespeople who have left me will come back!

Yesugai's former followers left and even took away Yesugai's animals.

Tiemuzhen went through many trials. Those who had abandoned him were worried that Tiemuzhen would take revenge on them one day. They wanted to kill him first.

He once hid in the forest for nine days and nights without food or drink. He was later captured but escaped when the guard was not looking.

With his intelligence and courage, Tiemuzhen escaped danger time and again, in the process developing an unbending and determined nature.

Later, he built up his tribe and ultimately united all the whole of Mongolia. He thus became Genghis Khan, meaning 'the emperor of the universe'.

Zhu Yuanzhang — the monk emperor

Zhu Yuanzhang, the founding emperor of the Ming Dynasty, was once a monk due to the poverty of his family when he was a youth. He later joined the rebel forces in overthrowing the Yuan Dynasty and established his empire, restoring China to Han rule.

Zheng He's travels to the West

The reign of the Ming Dynasty's third emperor – Ming Chengzu – was the dynasty's most glorious period. The emperor often sent envoys overseas to propagate the state's power. One of the largest -scale projects with far-reaching results undertaken was Zheng He's travels to the West. Zheng He was a court official and was also known as the Eunuch of Sanbao. From 1405 to 1433, he made seven trips to the West. He brought with him Chinese silk, porcelain, tea leaves, farming tools and many others in exchange for foreign rare treasures. Among his destinations were the Indo-Chine Peninsula, the

Malayan Peninsula, islands in the South China Sea, India, Persia, Arabia, the eastern coast of Africa and the Red Sea. In all, he visited more than 30 countries and regions.

The *Yongle Encyclopaedia*

During the reign of Yongle of the Ming Dynasty, Emperor Chengzu assembled a team of 2,000 people to compile the *Yongle Encyclopaedia*. The set comprised 11,095 volumes that included over 7,000 to 8,000 different titles. This was the largest collection of its kind in China. Today, only about 300 volumes have survived.

Wo Kou — Pirates

During the Ming Dynasty, Japanese pirates terrorised the southeastern coastal towns of China, burning, looting and killing. People called them *wo kou*. Some wicked landlords and evil merchants even colluded with these pirates, causing great harm to the people. In 1565, Ming generals Qi Jiguang and Yu Dayou led an army against the perpetrators and succeeded in destroying all the pirates.

End of the Ming Dynasty

In the twilight years of the Ming Dynasty, Li Zicheng raised a peasant army and occupied Beijing. The last Ming emperor, Emperor Chongzhen, hung himself at Mount Mei. General Wu Sangui allowed Qing troops through Shanhaiguan Pass to defeat Li Zicheng. This heralded the dawn of the Qing Dynasty.

> ### A Traitor for a Lady
> Folk belief has it that Wu Sangui betrayed his country to get back his beloved, Chen Yuanyuan, from one of Li Zicheng's men.

Ten Days in Yangzhou, Three Massacres of Jiading

To prevent the Qing army from progressing southwards, Shi Kefa formed a peasant militia in Yangzhou. He refused to surrender when Yangzhou fell and was killed. The Qing army then went on a 10-day rampage, killing tens of thousands, and this event was dubbed 10 Days in Yangzhou.

The Qing army met with fierce resistance from the people of Jiading as it pressed south. The townsfolk held fort for more than 80 days. After the city fell to the Qing army, more than 20,000 people were killed in three massacres. This incident came to be known as the Three Massacres of Jiading.

> ### Zheng Chenggong recovers Taiwan
> Zheng Chenggong is one of China's best-loved folk heroes. In 1662, he drove away the Dutch army that had occupied Taiwan for many years and used Taiwan as a base for the Qing resistence. He established a school in Taiwan and developed agriculture.

Qing Dynasty — China's last dynasty

In 1644, the Manchu army attacked and invaded the Ming Empire, beginning the period of Manchu rule in China. As the state of the Manchus was known as Qing, that era became known as the Qing Dynasty. The reigns of Kangxi, Yongzheng and Qianlong were the most powerful periods of the Qing Dynasty. The Qing Dynasty lasted close to 300 years and was overthrown in 1911, ending China's thousands of years of dynastic rule.

Nüzhen — Manchu

The predecessor of the Manchus was the Nuzhen people, living at the north and south reaches of Songhuajiang River and Heilongjiang River. In 1616, Nurhachi established the Later Jin Dynasty, which his son Huang Taiji changed to Qing Dynasty in 1636.

Kangxi   Yongzheng   Qianlong

Kangxi — China's wisest and most able emperor

The reign of Kangxi of the Qing Dynasty was the longest of any emperor in Chinese history. Kangxi is also hailed as the wisest emperor of all time. He subdued rebels and recovered Taiwan from the rule of Zheng Chenggong's descendants. During his reign, he was an able statesman who loved his people. He was interested in the development of the arts, and also sent for Western teachers to learn mathematics, geography, astronomy and Latin.

The Complete Collection in Four Treasures

Emperor Qianlong of the Qing Dynasty enlisted many scholars to compile the largest book collection in the world — *Si Ku Quan Shu* (*The Complete Collections in Four Treasures*).

The tumultuous 19th century

China began fighting the Opium War in 1840, thus progressing into modern history. The western powers used advanced warships and artillery to force open China's doors.

1839 – Destroying Opium at Humen
At Humen beach in Guangdong Province, Lin Zexu, the Qing government's imperial commissioner, destroyed over 1.1 million kilograms of opium confiscated from British and American smugglers.

1840 – The Opium War
British forces waged war on China. In 1842, China was defeated and signed the Treaty of Nanjing, the first of the unequal treaties, which ceded Hong Kong to the invaders.

1856 – The Second Opium War
To expand their occupation of China's land, British and French forces invaded China again. With China's defeat, she signed the Treaty of Tianjin with Britain, France, US and Tsarist Russia, and the Treaty of Aihun with Russia in 1858. China signed another unequal Treaty of Beijing with Britain, France and Russia in 1860.

1860 – Old Summer Palace in Flames
During the Second Opium War, British and French forces occupied Beijing and raided the Old Summer Palace. The forces looted many of the palace's treasures, documents and art pieces, and later set fire to the garden.

1884 – The Sino-French War
France invaded Vietnam to start a war with China. Though China won the war, it had to sign a humiliating Sino-French New Treaty in favour of French interests.

1887 – Sino-Portuguese Treaty of Beijing
A treaty was signed between Portugal and the Qing government, ceding Macao to Portuguese forces.

1894 – Jiawu Sino-Japanese War
Japan invaded Korea to provoke the Chinese navy and army into war. In1895, China signed the Treaty of Shimonoseki with Japan, giving Japan full control of Taiwan, Penghu Islands and the Liaodong Peninsula. Later, Russia, Germany and France interfered and China was forced to pay Japan more money to buy back Liaodong Peninsula.

1894 – Sino-US Treaty on Chinese Workers
This was a treaty that limited the rights of Chinese workers in America. It stipulated that the Chinese were not allowed to become American citizens.

1898 – Special Article on Expanding the Territory of Hong Kong
The British forced the Qing court to sign a treaty making Kowloon a British concession, with a term of 99 years. This led to the Germans, Russians, French and Japanese wanting a piece of China as well.

1900 – The Eight-Power Allied Army
Britain, USA, Germany, France, Russia, Japan, Italy and Austria combined forces to invade China and captured Tianjin and Beijing. China was forced to sign the 1901 Treaty, paying an indemnity of 450 million taels of silver. The Qing court guaranteed that anti-imperialist activities were prohibited and allowed the imperialist troops to station at points along the railway track between Beijing and Shanhaiguan Pass. Dongjiao Minxiang in Beijing was sealed off as the embassy area where no Chinese residents were allowed.

Lin Zexu Destroys Opium at Humen

In the 19th century, foreign opium was smuggled into China in largequantities.

China was gripped by an addiction to opium smoking. The Chinese became lazy and despondent.

If this goes on, not only will the economy suffer, in 10 years' time, the Qing empire will have no soldier fit enough to fight!

Imperial Commissioner Lin Zexu went to Guangzhou to implement a ban on opium.

Lin Zexu ordered all the foreign opium smugglers to hand the substance over. The foreigners began speculating on the issue.

He must be trying to keep all the profits for himself!

Hmph! Many officials not only collude with foreign traders, they are also addicts!

Submerge all the opium in seawater and add in raw cement. Throw them all into the sea!

After impounding the opium from the smugglers, Lin Zexu destroyed all the opium in public at Humen.

Lin Zexu also wanted the foreign traders to sign agreements, promising not to bring in anymore opium.

All opium smugglers will be sentenced to death!

After this feat at Humen, the foreign opium traders suffered a blow to their business. In the Opium War later, Lin Zexu was determined to fight the British invaders but was removed from duty before he could succeed in his goal.

The Taiping Heavenly Kingdom

While China was facing external aggression in 1851, a peasant movement broke out and lasted 15 years. Hong Xiuquan led the Jintian Uprising against the Qing government in Jintian Village, Guiping of Guangxi. He established the Taiping Heavenly Kingdom and called  himself Heavenly King. Hong Xiuquan visualised an ideal society where land, food, clothes and wealth were shared by all.

The Westernisation Movement

After witnessing the might of the Western powers, some Qing officials advocated learning to use the West's advanced production technology to safeguard and maintain the rule of the Qing court. They belonged to the Westernisation School and included people such as Zeng Guofan, Li Hongzhang, Zuo Zongtang and Zhang Zhidong. The main concerns of the movement were to establish military and civil industries, build modern schools, send scholars overseas, and train translators, military personnel and scientists.

The 1898 Reform Movement (Wuxu Bianfa)

The 1898 Reform Movement was a bid to save China. Emperor Guangxu accepted the proposals by Kang Youwei and Liang Qichao to reform the political, economic, cultural and military systems. The movement only lasted 103 days before it was suppressed by the Empress Dowager Cixi. She put to death six of the advocates – Tan Sitong, Kang Guangren, Yang Shenxiu, Yang Rui, Lin Xu and Liu Guangdi. They were known as the Six Wuxu Heroes.

Regency behind the screen

Empress Dowager Cixi was the true ruler during the reigns of Tongzhi and Guangxu. She began her regency from behind the screen after a coup she plotted in 1861, and held the reins of power in China for over 40 years.

Pu Yi – China's last emperor

Pu Yi was only three years old when he ascended the throne. In 1911, in the revolution led by Sun Yat-sen, the Qing court employed Yuan Shikai, who had great military power, to help fight the revolutionaries. However, Yuan Shikai collaborated with Sun Yat-sen to force Pu Yi to abdicate the throne. Pu Yi was only six years old then.

A Brief Chronology of Chinese History

夏 Xia Dynasty			About 2100 – 1600 BC
商 Shang Dynasty			About 1600 – 1100 BC
周 Zhou Dynasty	西周 Western Zhou Dynasty		About 1100 – 771 BC
	東周 Eastern Zhou Dynasty		770 – 256 BC
	春秋 Spring and Autumn Period		770 – 476 BC
	戰國 Warring States		475 – 221 BC
秦 Qin Dynasty			221 – 207 BC
漢 Han Dynasty	西漢 Western Han		206 BC – AD 24
	東漢 Eastern Han		25 – 220
三國 Three Kingdoms	魏 Wei		220 – 265
	蜀漢 Shu Han		221 – 263
	吳 Wu		222 – 280
西晉 Western Jin Dynasty			265 – 316
東晉 Eastern Jin Dynasty			317 – 420
南北朝 Northern and Southern Dynasties	南朝 Southern Dynasties	宋 Song	420 – 479
		齊 Qi	479 – 502
		梁 Liang	502 – 557
		陳 Chen	557 – 589
	北朝 Northern Dynasties	北魏 Northern Wei	386 – 534
		東魏 Eastern Wei	534 – 550
		北齊 Northern Qi	550 – 577
		西魏 Western Wei	535 – 556
		北周 Northern Zhou	557 – 581
隋 Sui Dynasty			581 – 618
唐 Tang Dynasty			618 – 907
五代 Five Dynasties	後梁 Later Liang		907 – 923
	後唐 Later Tang		923 – 936
	後晉 Later Jin		936 – 946
	後漢 Later Han		947 – 950
	後周 Later Zhou		951 – 960
宋 Song Dynasty	北宋 Northern Song Dynasty		960 – 1127
	南宋 Southern Song Dynasty		1127 – 1279
遼 Liao Dynasty			916 – 1125
金 Jin Dynasty			1115 – 1234
元 Yuan Dynasty			1271 – 1368
明 Ming Dynasty			1368 – 1644
清 Qing Dynasty			1644 – 1911
中華民國 Republic of China			1912 – 1949
中華人民共和國 People's Republic of China			1949 –

LANGUAGE AND NAMES

Legend has it that the written language was created by Cangjie, a subordinate of the Yellow Emperor. However, this is just a myth because the development of a written language is influenced by many social factors over a long time.

Before the written word was invented, people tied knots on strings and notched wood to make records. However, these methods could only record simple things such as the quantity of an item. Later, people began to draw objects to form meaningful symbols. Such pictograms were the earliest forms of the Chinese written word.

Although the written word was not invented by Cangjie solely, the myth highlights the ingenuity of the forefathers of the Chinese nation in seeking solutions to any difficulties they encountered. This development made life more convenient and spurred the development of the Chinese civilisation.

Cangjie and the written word

Cangjie was in charge of managing livestock and food supplies. As the animals and grain kept increasing, it became impossible to keep count. Hence, he made knots in different coloured strings to represent the numbers of different animals and food.

Seeing Cangjie's ability, the Yellow Emperor put him in charge of many more things. Cangjie racked his brains as strings were not sufficient now.

One day, Cangjie went hunting. He observed the animal footprints on the ground and got a revelation: "If one type of footprint represents one kind of animal, why don't I just indicate the different items with symbols?"

Hence, Cangjie began to come up with different symbols based on the shapes of animal footprints and the natural environment. Later, others also adopted these symbols and started to communicate with them.

Chinese Characters

The square block characters

The Chinese script is one of the oldest in the world. Each character is written by itself in a square block, hence the name 'square block characters'.

Chinese characters have three elements: form, pronunciation and meaning. Each character is an ideograph rather than a phonetic alphabet.

The structure of the Chinese characters can be divided into two types — single component characters and combination characters.

Most Chinese characters are combinations of several hundreds of components in various positions. As in the example below, the character '*kou*' (口) can be combined with other components in different positions to form new characters. '*Kou*' can be placed on the left or right, top or bottom:

chi	*zhe*	*kou*	*hao*	*gu*	*jing*
吃	哲	扣	号	古	京

Oracle bone inscriptions

Chinese characters were first derived from drawings. The earliest and fairly mature Chinese script was found during the Shang Dynasty. Oracle bone inscriptions were pictographs that looked very much like drawings. There was no paper at that time and men carved these words onto tortoise shells and animal bones. About 150,000 pieces of inscribed bones and shells were unearthed in the Yinshang region, and from these pieces, 1.6 million characters were found, of which there were 4,600 single characters. More than 1,000 characters have been deciphered.

This is the earliest form of writing — oracle bone inscription

The six categories of Chinese characters

The Han Dynasty created six ways of forming new characters — pictographs, indicative, associative compounds, picto-phonetic characters, synonymous characters and phonetic loan characters. The former four are ways to create characters while the last two are for character usage.

How Chinese characters were formed

The first Chinese characters were modelled after the shape of objects.

日 (sun)　　山 (mountain)

Another type is formed from two or more elements to convey a new meaning.

Example: *Xiu* 休 (rest) is formed from *ren* 人 (man) and *mu* 木 (wood), where the two characters combine to form a new character. It depicts a man leaning against a tree.

Punctuation marks can be used to modify the meaning of a character.

Example: A dot added to the character *dao* 刀 (knife) forms *ren* 刃 (edge of a knife), pointing to the sharp edge of the knife.

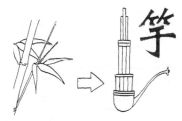

Alternatively, a radical representing the meaning and another representing the sound of the character may be combined. Ninety percent of Chinese characters are of this type.

Example: An ancient musical instrument called *yu* was made of *zhu* 竹 (bamboo). Hence, *zhu yu* 于 combine to form the character *yu* 竽.

Due to shifts in pronunciation over time, the sounds of many characters are now different from their phonetic radicals. For example:

妙 (*miao*)　　　沙 (*sha*)

Though *miao* and *sha* both share the same phonetic radical *shao* 少, they are pronounced differently.

The evolution of Chinese characters

Shell-and-bone style	Bronze Inscriptions	Small-seal style	Official style	Regular style
魚	魚	魚	魚	魚
鹿	鹿	鹿	鹿	鹿
鳥	鳥	鳥	鳥	鳥

The shell-and-bone style of Chinese writing goes a long way back. Over time, the strokes evolved from drawings to writing, from pictographs to symbols and from the complicated to simple. There were inscriptions on bronzeware in the shell-and-bone style during the Shang and Western Zhou Dynasties.

Before one can master the various writing styles in calligraphy, one should know the various strokes: dot, horizontal line, upstroke to the right, left-falling stroke, hook, bend, right-falling stroke and vertical line.

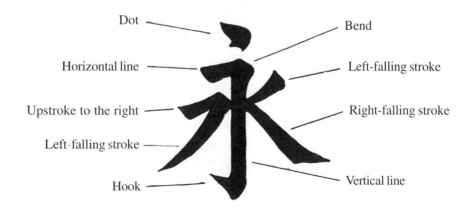

Dot — Bend
Horizontal line — Left-falling stroke
Upstroke to the right — Right-falling stroke
Left-falling stroke —
Hook — Vertical line

The eight strokes of the character *yong*

The order of strokes

In writing Chinese characters, there is an order that the strokes must follow.

Rule	Example	Order
heng comes before *shu*	*shi* (十)	一 十
pie comes before *na*	*da* (大)	一 ナ 大
from top to bottom	*duo* (多)	ク 夕 多
from left to right	*ni* (你)	亻 仁 你
from outside to inside	*yue* (月)	丿 刀 月
closing stroke last	*guo* (国)	冂 国 国
the middle before either side	*xiao* (小)	亅 小 小

Components and classifications

Pianpang 偏旁, or radicals, are the basic cells of composed characters. For example, the word *he* 河 is made up of the components 氵and *ke* 可.

Bushou 部首 refers to the *pianpang* that serve to classify the characters according to their structures. This is usually the first component of each character section in Chinese dictionaries. There are altogether 200 *bushous* such as 扌, 亻 and 氵.

Simplified Chinese and original complex characters

In 1956, the Chinese government announced the new Scheme for Simplifying Chinese Characters to make writing easier. The new characters are thus called *jiantizi* (simplified Chinese characters) or *jianti* while the traditional forms are called *fantizi* (original complex characters).

China and Singapore use the simplified characters whereas Taiwan, Hong Kong and Malaysia continue to use the complex characters.

Chinese Dictionaries

The earliest dictionary in China is the *Erya* which is classified according to the characters' meanings.

The Han Dynasty scholar Xu Sheng's book *Shuowen Jiezi* (*Definitions of Characters*) was the first dictionary that gave definitions and illustrated examples for the radicals of the six categories.

The famous *Kangxi Dictionary* of the Qing Dynasty has a collection of more than 47,000 characters.

The Chinese Language

Chinese, Common Language and Mandarin

The Chinese language originated from the Sino-Tibetan language family.

Putonghua 普通话 is the modern common language of the Chinese nation which uses the Beijing pronunciation as the standard. The basic dialect is the Beijing northern dialect and the grammar standard is based on the typical modern vernacular works.

Mandarin in mainland China is known as *putonghua* (common language), *guoyu* 国语 (national language) in Taiwan, and *huayu* 华语 (Chinese language) in Singapore and Malaysia.

Intonation

There are three main elements in Chinese pronunciation — consonant, vowel and tone.

The four tones are, the *yingping* (high and level tone), *yangping* (rising tone), *shangsheng* (falling-rising tone) and *qusheng* (falling tone). Due to these different tones, spoken Chinese has a musical sound.

Classical and Vernacular

Wenyanwen (classical) and *baihuawen* (vernacular) are two different styles of written Chinese.

Classical: A friend comes from afar, happy?
Vernacular: A friend is coming from afar, is that not a happy thing?

After the May 4th Movement in 1919, vernacular Chinese became the formal written Chinese.

Dialects

Chinese dialects are defined by geography, with each dialect used in a specific region. In China, the seven major dialects include the northern dialect, the Wu (Jiangsu) dialect, the Xiang (Hunan) dialect, the Gan (Jiangxi) dialect, the Hakka dialect, the Yue (Cantonese) dialect and the Min (Hokkien) dialect.

Terms

Ci 词, or terms, are the smallest language units. They can be used independently, for example:

Types of Terms	Description
Danyici	Terms with only one meaning
Duoyici	Terms with two or more meanings
Tongyinci	Homophones; words with similar sounds
Tongyici	Synonyms; words with similar meanings, eg. happy — elated
Fanyici	Antonyms; words with opposite meanings, eg. clean — dirty
Wailaici	Borrowed terms, eg. coffee, bus
Mingci	Nouns; names of people, objects or places, eg. Xiaoming, father, computer, Asia
Xingrongci	Adjectives; descriptive words, eg. beautiful, cheerful, sad
Dongci	Verbs; showing action or activity, eg. walk, run, laugh, cry
Liangci	Units of measurement

There are also other terms such as adverbs, auxiliaries, interjections and conjunctions.

Chengyu, or idioms, are commonly-used set phrases usually made up of four characters, such as *hujia huwei* (bully others by flaunting one's connections), *yidao liangduan* (sever all ties) and *baidu buyan* (never tire of something).

Yanyu, or proverbs, often come in paired conditional phrases. For example, *tianxia wu nanshi, zhi pa youxin ren* (where there is a will, there is a way) and *liu de qingshan zai, bu pa mei chai shao* (as long as you maintain your reserves, your livelihood is guaranteed).

Xiehouyu are spoken phrases with two parts. The first part is a riddle while the second part answers the riddle. Most people say only the first portion and imply the rest. For example, *nipusa guo jiang — zi shen nanbao* (The mud bodhisattva crossing the river — he can't even protect himself) and *roubaozi da gou — you qu wu hui* (throw a bun at a dog — it won't come back).

Guanyongyu are short and fixed spoken phrases that are easy to understand, such as *tianxiaode* (heaven knows), *paimapi* (currying favour) and *potianhuang* (unprecedented).

Names

It is composed of two parts: *nü* 女 (woman) and *sheng* 生 (birth) indicating that it is a woman who gives birth. This implies that in primitive times, China was a matriarchal society. Children knew who their mother was but not their father, and so they took their mother's surname. Later, as the Chinese developed into a patriarchal society, children began to take their father's surname.

女 + 生 = 姓

Creation of surnames

There are more than 8,000 Chinese surnames, of which only 200 to 300 are common. There are single character surnames like Zhang, Wang and Li, and two-character ones like Ouyang, Sima and Shangguan. The former are more common.

How did these surnames come about? There are several sources. Some were taken from a state, like Qi. There were also titles, such as Sima and Situ, which were ancient ministerial posts. Occupations were also possible options, so a person with the surname Tao might have ancestors who were potters. Some people also used the landmarks of their place of residence, such as Ximen 西门 (west gate), Liu 柳 (willow), and Chi 池 (pond).

> ### One Hundred Family Names
> The book entitled *One Hundred Family Names* was written during the Song Dynasty and has been widely circulated. The book contains a total of 494 surnames, which are categorised in a four-character word pattern such as "Zhao Qian Sun Li, Zhou Wu Zheng Wang" to make reciting easier. The book later became a textbook in rudimentary education.

Personal names

Parents usually give names that connote luck or carry good wishes. Boys tend to get names that denote strength and power, while girls have gentler names that connote beauty or virtue.

Most people have two-character names, but single character names are also common.

Common character

In some families, the children might share a common character in their names. For example, three sisters might be named Huiyun, Huizhen, and Huifen, with the common character being 'Hui'.

Pet names

Many people have pet names by which they are addressed as children, such as Xiaosanzi or Niu-niu.

Some naming practices used in the past

The Chinese had many interesting ways of choosing names back then. Just listen to these:
- "Since he's our third child, let's call him Xiaosanzi 小三子 (Little third son)."
- "Call him Wujiu 五九 (Five nine). I'm 22 and you're 23. The sum of 22 and 23 is 45. And 5 x 9 gives 45."
- "Hmm, doesn't he weigh seven *jin*? Let's call him Qijin 七斤 (Seven *jin*)."

Apart from the surname and given name, a second name, *zi* 字, was also given when a person came of age. He may also adopt one or more nicknames that reflect his interests, physical characteristics, achievements, or the place he lives in. For example, Zhuge Liang, the famous tactician of the Three Kingdoms, was addressed as Kongming and nicknamed Wolong (Crouching Dragon). Generally, a senior will introduce himself with his *ming* 名 (first given name). A junior will address his senior or his peer by the latter's *zi*.

However, a married Chinese woman may take her husband's surname, or put her husband's surname before her maiden surname. For example, you may address Wang-Li Huiyun as Mrs Wang or Madam Li.

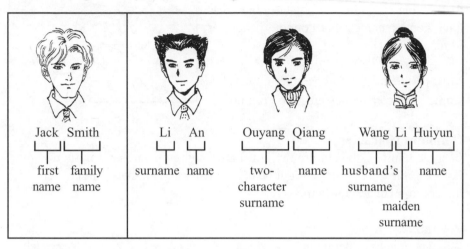

Jack Smith
first name / family name

Li An
surname / name

Ouyang Qiang
two-character surname / name

Wang Li Huiyun
husband's surname / maiden surname / name

Emperors' titles

Shihao 谥号 *(Posthumous honorific)*
Emperors, princes, dukes and high-ranking officials were given a title based on their achievements and moral character. A title with *wen* 文 or *wu* 武 is commendatory whereas one with *li* 厉 or *you* 幽 is derogatory.

Miaohao 庙号 *(Posthumous title)*
The founder of a dynasty would be given the title of Taizu 太祖, Gaozu 高祖 or Shizu 世祖 (*zu* 祖 means progenitor). Later emperors would be given posthumous titles such as Taizong 太宗, Shizong 世宗 or Shenzong 神宗 (*zong* 宗 means ancestor).

Nianhao 年号 *(Title of the emperor's reign)*
This is the name used to keep track of the years an emperor reigned. Some emperors might have more than one reign title, but by the Ming and Qing Dynasties, most emperors had only one, such as Yongzheng. The reign title may be used in place of the emperor's name or *miaohao*, as with Emperor Kangxi and Emperor Qianlong.

PHILOSOPHY AND RELIGIONS

China's main philosophies – Confucianism, Taoism, Legalist, Mohist and Strategist – all arose during the Spring and Autumn, and Warring States Periods. This was the Contention of the Hundred Schools.

The Chinese philosophies of not taking wealth won by unjust means, contentment in life, the transience of riches and interdependence of disaster and fortune came into being more than 2,000 years ago. These philosophies have become a unique feature of the Chinese nation.

The Contention of the Hundred Schools took place during the Spring and Autumn, and Warring States Periods. It was a time of war and upheaval. At the same time, it was also a time of great reforms. War overturned the old systems and new ones were developed. Rulers and aristocrats then enlisted the services of many intellectuals and scholars, who went to each kingdom, spreading their doctrines. The practice of taking in disciples was very popular and thus, numerous 'schools' sprang up, each with their own set of philosophies. People called them the Hundred Schools of Thought and labelled the frenzied situation the Contention of the Hundred Schools. It was a golden age for Chinese philosophy.

Among these schools were the Nine Philosophies and Ten Classes: The Nine Philosophies were Confucianist, Taoist, Positive and Negative Principles, Legalist, Logician, Mohist, Political Strategist, Eclectic, and Agriculturist, with Novelists forming the 10th Class.

A Hundred Philosophers and a Hundred Schools of Thought

The turbulent Warring States Period was a time of many drastic changes. Philosophers all had divergent opinions and perspectives, hence, there arose 'a hundred schools of thought' during this period.

Confucius

Confucius is the founder of the Confucian school. Also known as the Sage, he advocated ruling with benevolence and put strong emphasis on moral development.

Emperor Wu of the Han Dynasty was a strong proponent of the Confucian school, which became one of the pillars of Chinese society, dominating Chinese thought for over 2,000 years.

A great educator himself, Confucius felt that everyone should be given an equal opportunity to receive schooling. He stressed that students should learn how to think and not just go for rote learning.

After his death, his students compiled his teachings into *The Analects*, a classic of the Confucian teachings.

> **Confucius said:**
> There is joy in eating simply and sleeping anywhere. Status and wealth gained by illegitimate means are to me like fleeting clouds.

Mencius

Another representative figure of the Confucian school, Mencius is known as the Lesser Sage. He advocated benevolent governance wherein the citizens were above the ruler. The ruler should possess good morals to gain the respect of the people. Mencius also believed in the innate goodness of human nature.

Laozi

The founder of Taoism, Laozi wrote *The Classic of the Virtue of the Tao*. Containing 5,000 aphorisms, it is the Taoist scripture.

Laozi believed that the Tao formed the basis of the universe, the origin of all things. However, it is not inaction that he advocates but non-competitiveness and not compelling things to happen.

Stubborn and inflexible things break easily while pliant things flourish. Laozi advocated modesty, non-competitiveness, overcoming force with gentleness and retreating to advance.

Laozi's famous words

The universe is contradictory, interdependent and interrelated. When there is disaster, there may be happiness, and when there is happiness, disaster may be close by.

Zhuangzi

Zhuangzi is another major representative of the Tao. He was opposed to human endeavour and believed that nature should be allowed to take its course. Zhuangzi believed that true freedom in life was freedom from conditions. In the famous 'Zhuangzi Dreams of A Butterfly', Zhuangzi dreamt that he was a butterfly. When he awoke, he didn't know if he had dreamt he was a butterfly, or if the butterfly was now dreaming about being him.

Sunzi

Sunzi is an important figure in the art of war. *Sunzi's Art of War is* a seminal work of military writing. He mooted the concept of making one's enemy submit without the use of force while stressing that winning every battle was not the ideal strategy in warfare. Hence he stressed the importance of military intelligence to find out the strength of one's enemy. He believed that knowing one's enemy and knowing oneself would take one very far in warfare.

The dissemination of *Sunzi's Art of War*
During the Tang Dynasty, S*unzi's Art of War h*ad already been distributed in Japan. In the last hundred years, the book has been translated into many different languages including English, French, Russian and German. *Sunzi's Art of War* has also been applied in areas such as business and management.

Mozi

Mozi, the founder of the Mohist School, was born in a poor family and worked as a carpenter. His two main concerns were compassion and pacifism. He felt that wars were caused by the failure of people to love others as they loved themselves. The compassionate love that he

advocated knew no class differences; it was an all-embracing universal love. If one loved others, one would then be loved in turn. Mozi deemed war as the greatest ill which would only cause harm and pain.

Han Feizi

A key figure of the Legalist School, Han Feizi advocated the application of law (formal laws and regulations), tactics (ways to wield control) and power (political power) for the incumbent ruler. He believed that policies should be drafted in correspondence to the situation at hand and was against a stick-in-the-mud approach.

Central Tenets of Chinese Philosophy
Syncretism Between Heaven and Humanity

The ancients believed that heaven, earth and humanity were closely interrelated, having influence over one another. Thus, ancient Chinese philosophy held 'Heaven and Humanity as one', stressing the importance of the harmonious co-existence of humans and nature.

Yin, Yang and the Five Elements

Ancient Chinese philosophers saw two aspects to every phenomenon, and they used the concepts of yin and yang to explain the inner materialised powers that are mutually beneficial and conflicting. They regarded the yin and yang as the basic law of the universe and used the concepts to explain social phenomena.

The Five Elements – water, fire, wood, metal and earth – are believed to be the basic foundation on which the universe is built, with the five elements balanced in supporting and opposing each other.

The Book of Changes

The Book of Changes is an ancient book on divination. Based on the Eight Trigrams, it is used to predict cosmic phenomena and for divination.

As the title of the book implies, nothing in the cosmos remains constant. Everything is in the process of change. But these changes are ordered and sequential. For example, where there is prosperity, it will be followed by a decline. Where there are ups, there will be downs.

This school of thought has greatly influenced a wide spectrum of the Chinese psyche, from philosophy, medicine and religion to politics.

Every symbol is represented by either of the signs "_" or "_ _", or both. "_" is a symbol of yang and "_ _", a symbol of yin.

Traditional Chinese Ideologies

Loyalty and filial piety

Chinese ideology revolves around loyalty and filial piety. A person is filial to his family and loyal to his country.

Loyalty comprises love for the nation and home, and selflessness in protecting the family and fellow countrymen in its ideals. Hence, loyalty is the highest form of morality. Without loyalty, any other virtues are meaningless.

The centripetal force and close bonds that evolved from 'patriotism' has led to the unity of the Chinese nation.

Sacrificing oneself for a just cause

Humanity, justice and virtue are more precious than life. This mentality is demonstrated in the proverb, 'Rather be a shattered vessel of jade than an unbroken piece of pottery' (better to die in glory than live in dishonour), and for this reason, there has never been a shortage of idealists willing to die for their cause in Chinese history.

Mencius' fish and bear's paw

I love eating fish, but I also love eating bear's paw.
If I can't have both at the same time,
I'd rather give up the fish and take the bear's paw instead.
I cherish life, but I also live by morality and justice.
If I can't have both,
I'd rather give up life than abandon morality and justice.

The Golden Mean

The Golden Mean is the fundamental principle of Confucian ethics and the way to behave in society and towards people. It requires people to be impartial, take a neutral attitude, avoid extremes, defend justice and maintain absolute balance. Just as the string of a zither will snap if tuned too tightly, but would not produce a good sound if too loose, in dealing with matters and people, one must adopt appropriate behaviour and attitude, avoid overreaction, and take an objective and unbiased stand. This is the Chinese ideal of proper conduct.

The golden mean also reflects the spirit of magnanimity where all nationalities and nations should respect one another and coexist in harmony. With an open heart, there can be true cultural exchange.

Character and career-building

The Chinese believe in building one's character and also one's career. Their yearning to carve a niche for themselves reflects the Chinese desire to realise their ideals. Character-building in itself is incomplete unless they are able to apply what they have learnt to contribute to society and country.

Great Harmony

Great Harmony is an ideal or perfect society that the people of olden times used to pursue. Great Harmony resembles a large harmonious family where people get along peacefully with one another. Everyone in the society is taken care of and there is no such thing as crime and evil. Great Harmony was one of Confucius' earliest ideologies.

Diligence and perseverance

As the Chinese saying goes, 'A person who can take hardship is a notch above others.' To be able to suffer hardship and persevere are traits of the Chinese. This is the embodiment of the doctrine that 'one should always strive to be stronger'. This enthusiasm and optimism constantly drive the nation forward.

Religions and Faiths

Taoism

Taoism is a religion native to China, founded during the Eastern Han period. Taoism regards Laozi of the Warring States Period as the father of the faith. His book, *The Classic of the Virtue of the Tao*, forms the backbone of the Taoist faith. Taoists believe that only with a still heart and a life free from desires will one be able to truly achieve Tao.

Making pills of immortality

Attaining immortality is the highest attainment in Taoism. Followers of Taoism made pills from cinnabar, realgar and mercury, believing they would help them achieve immortality. Alternatively, cultivation of the spirit and *qigong* can also help one return to the way of the Tao ultimately.

The Tao of Five *Dou* of Grain

The earliest Tao sect formed was known as the Tao of Five *Dou* of Grain, founded by Zhang Ling of Eastern Han Dynasty. All new members of the sect had to offer five *dou* of grain which would be used in times of famine. Zhang Ling used the water in which the ashes of burnt talismans had been mixed to exorcise ghosts. To this day, this custom is still in practice. Followers of the Tao of Five *Dou* of Grain number in the tens of thousands. They regard Zhang Ling as the Heavenly Master.

Buddhism

Buddhism originated in India and spread to China during the late Western Han and early Eastern Han dynasties. There, it began to absorb Chinese elements, developing into many different branches. Examples included the Dhyana Sect, Pure Land Sect, the Lu Sect and the Fu Sect, with the Dhyana Sect wielding the most influence. The Dhyana Sect promotes cultivation through meditation. It was introduced into China by Bodhidharma, an Indian monk.

Tang Sanzang and the Buddhist scriptures

In the early Tang period, Xuanzang left for India to fetch the Buddhist scriptures. He studied them in India for 17 years and brought many volumes of Buddhist scriptures back to China. His contribution to the development of Buddhism in China is immense. One of the four great Chinese literary classics – *Journey to the West* – is based on his journey.

Islam

Islam was founded by Muhammad, an Arab, in the seventh century. It spread to China during the Tang Dynasty. Minority groups in China like the Uyghurs and the Kazaks are Muslims. Zheng He, the famous explorer of the Ming Dynasty, was also a Muslim.

Christianity

Christianity first spread to China during the early Tang Dynasty. But it did not leave a great impact until the Ming and Qing Dynasties. It was only after western missionaries combined western culture and science with Christianity that the faith made inroads in China.

The Three Major Worships

Heaven and earth, the ancestors, as well as sovereignty and teachers were the three major objects of worship in China.

Heaven and earth worship

In ancient Chinese belief, heaven and earth were limitless and all-encompassing, so heaven was referred to as 'Sovereign Heaven' whereas earth was known as 'Imperial Earth'. Together, they were called 'Sovereign Heaven and Imperial Earth'. They were omnipresent and omniscient, so the ancient people swore by them to demonstrate their sincerity.

Praying for rain

Good weather was vitally important to farmers. The Dragon King was believed to govern rain. Hence, when there was a drought, people would flock to Dragon King temples with offerings or carry his statue in a grand parade to pray for rain.

Ancestor worship

Respecting one's ancestors is very important to the Chinese. Ancestor worship is to ask for protection and blessings from one's dead relatives.

In the early years of the Zhou Dynasty, ancestor worship was codified. Thereafter, everyone from government officials and commoners started to worship ancestors.

Ancestor worship can take place in many ways: praying at home, with the clan, orat the temple, sweeping tombs on special anniversaries, etc.

The ancestral tablet

Descendants treat ancestral tablets as places where the souls of the dead ancestors rest, and pray to these tablets. Tablets are usually made of wood and are often called 'wooden gods'.

Worshipping sovereignty and teachers

Sovereignty refers to emperors while teachers are the personages who were examples for all. They include Confucius and Lord Guan.

Confucius worship

A great philosopher and educator, Confucius had tremendous influence on China. Emperors of various dynasties have given Confucius various posthumous titles and organised Confucius worshipping activities. Confucius was highly regarded among the common people as well, with temples to him everywhere. Children must visit to pay their respects to him before starting school.

Worshipping Lord Guan (Guan Gong)

A famous character from the Romance of the Three Kingdoms. Lord Guan embodies loyalty and patriotism, and is a symbol of traditional moral ethics. During the Qing Dynasty, Lord Guan was given the title 'Holy Great Emperor' and honoured as the warrior god to Confucius' literary god. Lord Guan temples are common in and outside China and people pray to him not just for protection from harm or evil spirits, but even for wealth!

Patron saints of various trades

Lord Guan is also the patron saint for many trades such as pawnbrokers, gilders and textile merchants.

Among the Chinese trades, the founder of the trade is also worshipped. It is believed that the founder will protect the business of his disciples, blessing them with prosperity and wealth. For example, Shennong is the patron saint of the medical field, Lu Ban showers blessings on the construction industry and Cai Lun protects those in the paper manufacturing trade.

Other Deities

Mazu

Mazu is the protector of the seas, well-loved by coastal dwellers in China and beyond. According to legend, Mazu was a lady named Lin Moniang who lived in Putian, Fujian Province during the Song Dynasty. She saved many fishermen from disaster at sea. There are many places with Mazu temples where fishermen pray before going to sea.

The Kitchen God

The Kitchen God is the deity in charge of the stove. He protects the family and records the good and bad deeds of each family member to report to the heavenly court. The Jade Emperor would then mete out rewards and punishments accordingly.

Every 23rd or 24th day of the eight lunar month, people would offer him candied melon so that he would only be able to say sweet things about the family.

Fengshui

For the ancients, wind (*feng*) and water (*shui*) were always in flux, creating many opportunities. Seizing these opportunities would bring good fortune. *Fengshui* was originally a study of astronomy and geography, based on their perception of the environment and their concept of order.

The study gradually extended to one's residence — its structure, layout; and the geographical features around one's tomb. These formed the basis of a form of fortune-telling to predict good or ill fortune.

In *fengshui*, there is propitious land as well as ominous land. The mountains, rivers and wind direction around a residence or a tomb have direct bearing on the family's fortunes. Thus, a geomancer (*fengshui* master) is always consulted when building houses or tombs.

The Story of Mazu — Goddess of the Sea

During the Northern Song Dynasty, on Meizhou Island near Meizhou Bay in Putian, Fujian Province, a girl was born to the Lin family.

How strange, the baby doesn't cry at all. Let's call her Moniang*!

Growing up by the sea, Moniang was an excellent swimmer who could interpret the tides and understand astronomy.

At 16, she retrieved a divine bronze talisman from a well, which she used to treat the people's ailments.

When boats sank at sea, she would swim out and save the people from drowning.

One day, she fell asleep while weaving at home.

I'm so sleepy!

Save us!

In her dream, she was at sea and saw her father's boat sinking.

Moniang jumped into the sea and grabbed her brother, holding on to her father's sleeve with her teeth as she swam towards shore.

* Silent lady.

53

Moniang, wake up!

Mother...

As she opened her mouth to talk, she let go of her father's sleeve and he was swept away.

!

Mother, Brother and Father are in trouble!

Alarmed, Moniang woke up.

Trouble! Old Sir and Young Master have met with a mishap at sea. Only Young Master was saved. Old Sir is nowhere to be found!

A little later, bad news came.

Moniang rushed out to sea to search for her father. After three days, she carried her father's dead body home.

After bidding her family farewell, she left on a cloud for heaven.

Later, sailors caught in storms claimed to have seen Moniang, carrying a red lantern. As long as they steered towards the red light, the boat would be safe.

Moniang became known as Mazu or Goddess of the Sea.

The Jade Emperor

The Jade Emperor is believed to be the highest authority in heaven.

According to legend, Heaven appointed the Great White Star to select a virtuous and talented man to rule heaven, earth and hell. He transformed himself into a beggar and came to earth.

He came to Zhang Bairen's home.

Come in quickly!

I haven't eaten in three days!

Zhang Bairen prepared some food but the beggar snubbed them.

Why is there no meat and wine?

After he got meat and wine, the beggar wanted even more. Zhang Bairen patiently tried to meet the beggar's demands.

The beggar stayed on for almost half a month, but Zhang Bairen continued to treat him amicably. The beggar then revealed his true self.

I want to drink ginseng soup.

Ha, ha! You're the one I'm looking for!

Thus Zhang Bairen went up to heaven to become the emperor. He kept the three realms in perfect order and was well loved by all. As he was as pure as white jade, he was named the Jade Emperor.

Heaven Official Grants Fortune

There are Three Officials; the Heaven Official, Earth Official and Water Official. The Heaven Official brings fortune, the Earth Official absolves guilt, while the Water Official rids disasters. Their birthdays fall on the 15th day of the first, seventh and 10th lunar months respectively, and are collectively known as 'San Yuan Festival'.

They first appeared during the Eastern Han Dynasty, when Zhang Lin and Zhang Jiao, who were Taoist leaders, wrote the names of their patients on three pieces of paper. One was burnt, the second was buried in the earth and the third sunk in water to absolve the sins of the sick and let them recover.

A legend tells that they were actually three brothers born to a man named Chen Zishou. Chen had married three daughters of the Dragon King and each of them had a son. These three sons were then named the Three Officials and they were bound to take care of the earth's disasters and fortunes.

The most well known is the Heaven Official. He receives many offerings and prayers on the 15th day of the first lunar month from people who ask for his blessings.

CUSTOMS AND PRACTICES

Whenever there is a special event in one's life journey, such as a wedding, birth, birthday and even death, the Chinese will make sure it is an event to remember. Though birth is a cause for celebration, being able to experience a full life and die peacefully can be congratulated too. This shows the Chinese people's love for life and optimistic attitude.

The Chinese love the colour red. According to legend, this custom was already prevalent among the upper cave men more than18,000 years ago. They discovered that the blood that flowed in humans was red, and blood influenced life. Excessive loss of blood would lead to death. Hence, they believed that red objects were sacred. When loved ones died, red minerals were scattered onto the corpse in the hope that they could be revived.

From this association of red with life, the Chinese preference for red thus developed.

There are also physical and chemical factors behind the love for red. Red stimulates the brain into feeling exhilarated and happy. Therefore, the Chinese like to use red during happy occasions to enliven the atmosphere.

The red packet (*hongbao*) is derived from this love for all things red. It is given as a congratulatory note at almost all celebrations, such as weddings, month-old events and birthdays.

Red is an auspicious colour, hence it is taboo to use red during funerals. However, in some places, it is considered lucky for someone to live to a ripe old age. Women who have lived to great age are dressed in red at their funerals to honour their passing.

Wedding Practices

In olden days, marriages were arranged by parents and planned by matchmakers. Children had no say at all. Preparations for a wedding began when a family sent a matchmaker to another family to propose marriage. The two persons' horoscopes were then compared to see if they were compatible. The final decision lay with the parents.

Betrothal gifts

Once the match is agreed to, the bridegroom's family will send gifts to the bride's family to confirm the match. Once the betrothal gifts are accepted, the match cannot be lightly called off.

Bridal dowry

The bridal dowry is what the bride brings with her from her family to her husband's home. In the past, the value of the dowry affected her status in the family.

Three matchmakers and six proofs

Traditionally, a match is not confirmed until the engagement ritual is sealed with 'three matchmakers and six proofs'. The six proofs are an abacus, a measuring vessel, a ruler, a pair of scissors, a weighing balance, and a mirror.

Six courtesies

The six courtesies are: the marriage proposal, asking for names, praying for good fortune, sending betrothal gifts, extending invitations and welcoming the bride. Most modern Chinese couples now marry at their own free will and adopt Western practices, but they still retain some traditions, such as offering tea to their parents.

Welcoming the bride

In those days, the bride would be fetched to her husband's house in a sedan chair. On the way there, there would be a loud procession of drums and trumpets, signalling her arrival.

Bowing to Heaven and Earth

Afterwards, the bride and groom had to bow to Heaven and Earth, to their parents and to each other during the wedding ceremony before they were truly considered married.

Tea ceremony

Next, the couple proceeds to the groom's place. The newlyweds then offer tea to the elders of the groom's family. By drinking the tea, the elders show their acceptance of the bride as a new member of the family.

Modern Chinese Weddings

Although most Chinese now pick their own spouses, many still feel a marriage, even legally registered, is only 'real' after the traditional ceremony. A modern Chinese wedding is as follows:

Marriage proposal: The bridegroom's family will propose marriage to the bride's family. The details of the wedding will also be discussed.

Wedding gifts: The bridegroom's family will present gifts — traditionally a red packet, candles, jewellery, cakes, sweets, pig's trotters, chicken, fruit and wine — to the bride's family, who will usually return some of the gifts.

Wedding invitations: The bride's family will deliver the invitations together with the cakes from the bridegroom's family to their family and friends.

Brushing of hair: On the eve of the wedding, both bride and bridegroom will have their hair brushed at their own respective homes by someone who has a living spouse and many children and grandchildren.

Picking up the bride: The bridegroom will go to the bride's family home with his male entourage to receive the bride. The bride's younger brother or a young male relation will open the car door for the bridegroom.

Barricade by the bride's entourage: The bride's female friends and relations will lock the gate and demand a generous red packet or throw tough questions at the bridegroom before they let him into the house.

Tea ceremony: Next, the couple will proceed to the bridegroom's house to offer tea to his elders. (The tea ceremony for the bride's family may be carried out after this or just before the wedding dinner.)

Wedding banquet: The wedding banquet will be held in the evening for relatives and friends.

The bride returning to her parents' home: The newlyweds will pay a visit to the bride's parents three days after the wedding, or on the next day.

Red double happiness

The double-happiness character is often pasted on doors and windows, and even embroidered on pillows and blankets.

Distributing red eggs

In some places, red eggs are distributed whenever there is a wedding. Whether you are a relative, friend or even a total stranger, you may ask the bride for a red egg.

Birth Customs

The Chinese have this saying: Of the three unfilial acts, the worst is the failure to produce children. Childbearing is a duty that has strong moral overtones. To have many children and grandchildren is considered good fortune.

One-month confinement period

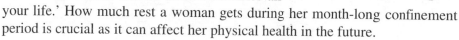

Chinese women observe a one-month confinement period after giving birth. This is a custom unique to the Chinese and has been in existence for a long time, and is still practised today. For a month after giving birth, a woman has to take special care of herself by keeping warm, reducing air in the stomach and taking tonics. An old adage says: 'Follow the rules of the confinement and be freed of worries all your life.' How much rest a woman gets during her month-long confinement period is crucial as it can affect her physical health in the future.

Full-month celebrations

When the baby is one month old, some families host a dinner to entertain friends and relatives. Red hard-boiled eggs will be distributed too.

An odd number of eggs will be distributed if it is a boy and an even number if it is a girl. Friends and relatives usually give a red packet in return. They may also give presents like baby food, articles for daily use or jewellery.

The 12 Animal Signs

The Chinese mark the years by the 10 Heavenly Stems and 12 Earthly Branches. For ease of recollection, they then match 12 animals to the 12 Earthly Branches. These 12 animals are arranged in this order: Rat, Ox, Tiger, Rabbit, Dragon, Snake, Horse, Goat, Monkey, Rooster, Dog and Pig.

By the Eastern Zhou Dynasty, the 12 animals were linked to the year in which one was born. They became the 12 animal signs. When a Chinese baby is born, the animal sign of that year would be his animal sign. For example, those born in 1998 are tigers and those born in the year 2000 are dragons.

Animal signs and astrology

Originally, the 12 animal signs were only a means of recording the years, but as time passed it developed into a system for divining one's fortune. Marriage partners could be picked based on the compatibility of their animal signs.

For example, the goat and the tiger are incompatible, as it would be like 'delivering the goat into the tiger's mouth'.

The Heavenly Stems are aligned with the Earthly Branches to make a series of 60 signs. The signs are used to denote the year, month, day and time. When one cycle ends, a new one will begin.

They are a system of signs for distinguishing different points of a sequence. The Heavenly Stems consist of 10 signs and the Earthly Branches, 12 signs.

Birthday Celebrations

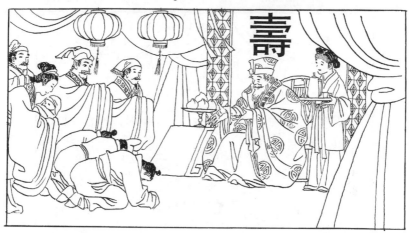

Among the traditional Chinese, only a person who is 60 years old or older has the privilege of celebrating his birthday. In Chinese thought, the Heavenly Stems and Earthly Branches make a full circle in 60 years. Those who are 60 would have completed this full cycle so they are no longer ordinary people. They now enjoy the same respect shown to the ancestors. On their birthdays, their children and grandchildren would extend their best wishes to them.

The numbers 9 and 10 have a special significance. 'Nine' is important because it is the largest single-digit number and also sounds like the word for longevity. Thus, when a person's age has a number 9 or is a multiple of 9, a big celebration would be planned. 'Ten' is regarded as a complete set and ages in multiples of tens are known as 'whole birthdays'. A person who has reached 80 is a wonder, so the 80th birthday celebration will be a big bash!

Longevity wine
Wine 酒 sounds like longevity 久, hence a gift of wine serves to wish the person a long life.

Longevity noodles
Long noodles represent long life. Care must be taken not to cut the noodles when cooking.

Birthday peaches
Usually, flour peaches are used as a substitute for fresh peaches.

Death Customs

The funeral

When parents or elders pass away, the children will usually try their best to arrange a decent funeral. 'Be filial to your elders when they are alive and mourn their passing when they die' is a Confucian teaching on filial piety.

The funeral wake

During the funeral, the body is placed in the mourning hall for relatives and friends to pay their last respects.

Visitors bring wreaths, banners with elegiac couplets written on them and cash contributions in white envelopes.

The bereaved family distributes red threads or red packets, each containing a coin, to friends and relatives so that they would return home safely.

Sombre colours should be worn at the wake to show respect to the dead.

Mourning clothes

The family members wear mourning clothes. The different colours of the mourning clothes show the relationship of the living to the deceased. Sons, daughters and daughters-in-law wear black and white. Grandsons and granddaughters wear blue.

Mourning band

The small piece of cloth pinned on the sleeve is known as a mourning band. This shows that the person wearing it is in mourning. If the person who has passed away is a man, the band is pinned on the left sleeve. If the deceased is a woman, the band is pinned on the right sleeve. The mourning band is usually worn for 49 to 100 days. During the mourning period and the period when the mourning band is worn, mourners must wear sombre colours. Colourful clothes are avoided.

Modern Chinese Funerals

The funeral of an elder is very important to the Chinese people. Below is a list of the general proceedings:

Death certificate: Obtain a certificate of death for the deceased.

Deathbed vigil: Before the passing of an elder at home, the family members will keep a vigil at the deathbed.

Announcement of death: The death is announced to friends and family. The time and venue of the wake is also usually placed in the obituary page of the local newspaper.

Mourning clothes: Family members of the deceased will wear mourning clothes based on their relation to the latter. In the past, family members will wear the mark of mourning for a period of time after the funeral. Nowadays the mourning clothes are burnt right after the burial or cremation.

Funeral wake: This normally lasts from three to seven days so that friends and relatives may attend the wake. The funeral rites also differ from family to family depending on their faith. For a Buddhist or Taoist funeral, monks or priests will conduct the funeral rites, while a Christian or Catholic funeral will have a church pastor or elder say the prayers.

Funeral procession: The deceased will be carried in the coffin to the burial grounds or crematorium, usually accompanied by a band.

Spirit tablet: The photo and spirit tablet of a late elder is placed on an altar at home or in the temple so family members can offer incense and offerings.

Auspicious Symbols

Dragon

The Chinese often refer to themselves as descendants of the dragon, and the dragon is a symbol of the Chinese nation. Chinese dragons first appeared in ancient times on totems. When all the tribes were united, they combined the figures of animals they had carved on their totems to form a new mythical creature, the dragon. The dragon later became the symbol of power, and the common people came to worship the Dragon King.

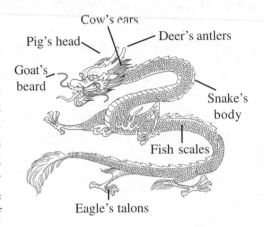

Cow's ears
Pig's head
Deer's antlers
Goat's beard
Snake's body
Fish scales
Eagle's talons

Phoenix

The phoenix is the mythical king of the birds, and is also an imaginary creature. The phoenix is looked upon as a symbol of benevolence, virtue and peace.

The dragon and phoenix are usually paired in wedding decorations as an auspicious symbol.

Kirin

The Chinese equivalent of the unicorn, the kirin represents unity and peace. Later, it was used to describe people of extraordinary abilities, so a clever child might be called 'the son of a kirin'. It is believed that the kirin will bestow children on childless couples who have high moral character. According to legend, a kirin appeared when Confucius was born.

Tortoise

The tortoise is an auspicious animal that represents long life and is said to be able to predict fortune or calamity, so shamans of ancient times used empty tortoise shells for divination.

Lion

The lion is the king of beasts and is often described as the incarnation of power. The ancient Chinese placed a pair of stone lions at the entrances of palaces and government offices to ward off evil.

Crane

According to legend, the crane can live for a thousand years. People often wish *he shou* or *he ling* (crane longevity) to people celebrating their birthdays.

Magpie

Magpies are auspicious birds that bring good news. They are also known as 'birds of joy'. People believe that magpies have the ability to forecast.

Bat

The Chinese character for bat *fu* has the same sound as prosperity. It is a symbol of happiness. There are many auspicious patterns that use the bat as a decorative design. Five bats would normally be used to represent the five blessings — longevity, fortune, safety, virtue and a peaceful passing.

Auspicious flowers

- The evergreen pine, bamboo and plum tree represent steadfastness and noble friendship.
- The peony symbolises fame and wealth.
- *Furong* (hibiscus) sounds like the words wealth and glory.
- The lotus is the gentleman's flower as it grows out from the mud, pure and unstained.

Taboos in Speech

Personal questions — Refrain from asking new acquaintances personal questions like age and salary.

Gesticulating — It is considered rude to point at people with your finger when you are talking.

Salutation — Avoid calling people 'hey'. Address the person by name. If the person is a stranger, you may use titles such as Mister, Miss and Madam.

Word choices — Avoid words that may be deemed insulting to the person you are speaking with, such as 'pig' for a fat person or 'bamboo' for a thin person.

Taboo Names

In ancient times, a certain type of taboo in names was practised. Any characters in the name of an emperor, elder, ancestor, sage or official that occurred in other terms had to be replaced. For example, Emperor Tang Taizong's name was Li Shimin. So during the Tang Dynasty, '*shi*' (age or era) became '*dai*' and '*min*' (people) became '*ren*'.

Officials may set fires, but the people may not even light lamps

There was a magistrate called Tian Deng during the Song Dynasty. He was especially particular about people using his name.

You may not use the word '*deng*' (lamp) or characters with the same sound.

Do not say 'light the lamp' (*dian deng*). You have to call it 'light the fire'.

On the 15th day of the first lunar month, lanterns were put on display as was the tradition.

To avoid the use of '*deng*', notices put up had this sentence in them: "The people may set fires for three days."

Tsk! The magistrate may set fires but the people can't even light a lamp!

This phrase was later used to describe people who do all kinds of evil but who deny other people their rights.

FESTIVALS

China has such a long history and culture that its festivals are plentiful. The whole nation celebrates the Lunar New Year, Lantern Festival and Dragon Boat Festival together. Festivals such as the Dexterity-Imploring Day (Cowherd and Weaving Maid's Meeting), Mid-Autumn Festival and Double Ninth (Chong Yang) Festival highlight family bonds. The Clear Brightness Festival (Qing Ming), Cold Food Festival (day before Qing Ming) and the Hungry Ghosts Festival are unusual occasions that the living and dead celebrate together.

Many Chinese festivals originated more than 5,000 years ago. The festivals are passed down from generation to generation of dragon descendants and bond the Chinese who live in different parts of the world.

The Chinese value family ties, hence they place special importance on social dealings and festivals that call for reunions. Festivals indirectly strengthened such familial bonds. "Family is greatly missed on festivals". Whenever a festival arrives, those who are away from home would always think of their loved ones.

Besides family reunions, Chinese traditional festivals often revolve around the worshipping of ancestors. On the eve of Lunar New Year, ancestors must be prayed to, and tombs must be swept during Clear Brightness Day. Through such ancestral worship, people will learn more about their ancestors and lineage, thus increasing the bond of the family and nation.

Some festivals have changed entirely in meaning due to the passage of time.

Chinese festivals embody the cultural characteristics and spirit of the nation. Through such festivals, people will gain deeper understanding of their own roots.

Lunar New Year

The Lunar New Year, also known as the Spring Festival, is the most important Chinese festival. It takes place from the first day to the 15th day of the first lunar month.

Living in the agricultural society of the past meant that everyone was busy working on the farm all day, and there were few opportunities for the whole family to meet except for weddings and funerals. Hence this period was set aside for family and friends to get together for dinner and to socialise, and over the years, this has developed into the custom of celebrating the new year.

Moreover, in the poor farming communities of those times, the common people had to live frugally, so this festival was one of the few occasions when they could feast on delicacies. Thus the Lunar New Year has always been a time of much festivity and merriment.

Spring-cleaning

Before the Spring Festival, every household will undergo a major clean-up where every corner of the house is cleaned to usher in the new year. When the job is done, all brooms will be put away. It is said to prevent one's wishes from being swept away.

I'll take out the rubbish.

Reunion dinner

The night before the Lunar New Year is known as the Lunar New Year's Eve. The whole family will gather and enjoy the reunion dinner together. As the Chinese people emphasise the family unit, the reunion dinner is considered the most important meal of the year. Married children and those who are overseas will try to come home for the reunion dinner.

Staying up late (*shou sui*)

The custom of staying up all night on the eve of the Lunar New Year to usher in the new year is called *shou sui*.

Red packet (*hongbao*)

On the eve of the Lunar New Year, the elders will give the children red packets, which the children will place under their pillows and open on New Year's Day.

It is customary for married people to give red packets to those who have yet to get married. The significance of the red packet is not in the amount of money it contains. Rather, it is a symbol of celebration, well wishes and good fortune.

Dragon dance and lion dance

Legend has it that dragons are in charge of rain. The dragon dance takes place during Lunar New Year celebrations to wish for a year of good rain. On the other hand, the lion dance is believed to ward off evil and carry with it all things auspicious.

Firecrackers

Lighting firecrackers was carried out to ward off evil ghosts. Also, the loud crackling of firecrackers served to liven up the atmosphere of celebration.

Lunar New Year visits

On the first day of spring, everyone will don their new clothes and visit their relatives and friends to wish one another a Happy New Year. New Year snacks and delicacies will also be served to guests.

Exchanging mandarin oranges

In the southern region of China as well as the Southeast Asian region, people will bring along two or four mandarin oranges when they visit friends and relatives during the Lunar New Year. In the Cantonese dialect, the mandarin orange sounds like gold. Therefore, the giving of mandarin oranges is likened to the giving of gold. The host will also return the guest the same number of mandarin oranges. Married daughters will usually visit their own parents on the second day of the Lunar New Year.

Group visitation

In recent years, companies and social organisations also conduct group visitations during the Lunar New Year.

On the seventh and eighth days, Chinese in the Southeast Asian region like to eat 'rainbow *yusheng*'. It's a special dish made of shredded vegetables, carrots, raw fish slices, and topped with sauces. Prior to serving, people would toss the ingredients together, mixing them up with their chopsticks while saying auspicious words.

Toss! Toss! Toss up good fortune and prosperity!

Meanings behind Chinese New Year goodies

Niangao (New Year cake)
Represents an increase in status every year.

Spring rolls
Symbolises good harvest and prosperity.

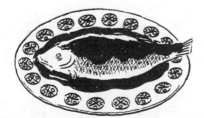

Fish (*yu*)
Symbolises hope for surplus every year.

Dumplings
Shaped like ancient gold ingots, they are therefore called Fortune God Dumplings.

New Year decorations

There is a kind of painting in China which is known as *nianhua* 年画 (New Year picture). The common folk will paste these pictures on their doors or walls during the Lunar New Year to mark the auspicious festival. These pictures will remain until they are replaced with new ones the following New Year. The earliest *nianhuas* were pictures of door gods used to ward off misfortune or evil.

Paper cuttings

There is another type of *nianhua* which is not called *nianhua* but *chuanghua* 窗花 (window flowers). It is a form of paper cutting and has a long history. The womenfolk in the northern part of China would gather together to do this craft just before the New Year. A pair of scissors was all they needed to cut out pretty and intricate designs that were pasted on the windows.

Spring couplets

During the New Year, spring couplets are another favourite decoration that people will put up. Spring couplets are also known as matching couplets. They are written on paper and cloth or carved on bamboo, wood and pillars. The couplets have to match each other in terms of presentation and content. Spring couplets were already seen during the Five Dynasties. By the Song Dynasty, it was a common feature and remains so to this day.

15th Night of the First Lunar Month (Lantern Festival)

The 15th night of the first lunar month is the first night of a full moon, hence it is also known as the Yuanxiao Festival. In Chinese, *yuan* means beginning and the first. This full-moon night is also known as a Lovers' Festival. On this day, the family will come together to eat *tangyuan* which symbolises completeness and happiness. It carries the same significance as the reunion dinner. This night is therefore also known as a minor Lunar New Year. It is generally accepted that this night marks the end of the Lunar New Year festivities.

Tangyuan
Also known as *yuanxiao*, these glutinous balls are placed in syrup. They symbolise reunion, harmony and sweetness.

Admiring lanterns and solving lantern riddles
The custom of admiring lanterns on the 15th night of the first lunar month started in the Yuan Dynasty. Lantern riddles were written on colourful lanterns, which some called Lantern Tigers. So solving lantern riddles was also known as shooting the lantern tiger.

Clear Brightness (Qing Ming) Festival

Legend has it that the Qing Ming Festival had its origins in the Han Dynasty. It acquired its name as the weather during the third lunar month was clear and bright, but it only became a festival during the Tang Dynasty. Originally, only the Cold Food Festival was celebrated, and the custom of sweeping tombs at this time only came into practice during the Tang Dynasty.

In ancient times, family clans and public organisations would conduct rites at graveyards or morgues to pray to their ancestors and remember the dead.

As the use of fire was prohibited during the Cold Food Festival, the Tang emperors would carry out the gifting of fire at that time. When the court session ended, an elm bough was lit and handed to the emperor, who would then bestow the branch on his officials as a new fire. Though the fire would be out by the time the officials reached home, they would leave the branch at their doorposts. During the Song Dynasty, the branch was replaced by a huge candle. Thus, the fire lit during the Qing Ming Festival is also known as new fire.

Tomb sweeping
On Tomb-Sweeping Day, people would clean the tombs of their ancestors and leave five-coloured papers to show that they had been there.

Kite-flying
As the Qing Mming Festival falls in the third lunar month which is a time of clear skies and wind, there would be kite-flying followed by tomb sweeping. As the wind direction after the Qing Ming period is unpredictable, there is a saying that kite-flying ends with the Qing Ming Festival. The act of flying the last kite is known as flying the broken sparrow hawk.

Sweeping the tomb

In olden days, pieces of five-coloured paper were placed on the grave with a stone put on top as a paperweight. It indicated that someone had visited the grave, and that it had not been abandoned.

Weeds on the tomb were pulled out and repair work was done where necessary. Then, the grave was covered with more earth and twigs of willow were stuck on it.

One should bow while burning joss paper.

Usually, the family would bring some food and wine as offerings to the ancestors.

Cold Food Festival

In ancient times, the Cold Food Festival was an important festival. It commemorated Jie Zitui of the Spring and Autumn and the Warring States Period. The Cold Food Festival fell one or two days before the Qing Ming Festival. On this day, no fire was to be lit. The people could only drink cold water and eat cold food. This festival originated around the Early Zhou Dynasty or the Spring and Autumn Period. During the Tang Dynasty, the people changed their focus to the Qing Ming Festival and the Cold Food Festival gradually became forgotten.

Dragon Boat Festival

The fifth day of the fifth lunar month is the Dragon Boat Festival. As that day falls between spring and summer, the weather is warmer and people fall sick easily. So it is called the poisonous month or the evil month.

Xionghuang wine (red orpiment)
On this day, the entire family must drink some Xionghuang wine, which is believed to be an detoxicant that is able to kill germs, relieve swelling and relieve heatiness. Hence, there is a popular proverb which goes, 'After drinking Xionghuang wine, all your illnesses will go away'.

Some also splash the wine around the house to prevent snakes from entering, while others write the word 'king' on a child's forehead with the wine.

Calamus (*changpu*) and Chinese mugwort (*baiai*)
Calamus is a stimulant and has anti-bacterial properties. Chinese mugwort is used to dispel dampness and colds, disperse phlegm, alleviate inflammations, and repel mosquitoes and houseflies. During the Dragon Boat Festival, people tie these plants on the door to ward off evil spirits.

The children would also wear fragrant pouches filled with the leaves of the *lingzhi* (glossy *ganoderma*).

The story behind dumplings and dragon boats

Dragon boat racing is a well-loved international sporting event, with more than 50 nations around the world taking part in the races each year.

According to legend, the tradition of eating dumplings and racing dragon boats began to commemorate Qu Yuan, a great patriotic poet during the Warring States period. A loyal citizen of Chu who had been banished because of slander, he plunged into the Gulao River in grief upon learning that the capital of Chu had fallen to the Qin army. The people rowed out in boats to try to save him, sounding drums to scare the fish away. They failed to recover his body, and threw rice wrapped in bamboo leaves into the river to feed the fish so that they would not eat Qu Yuan's body. Dragon boat races and rice dumplings thus became a tradition.

Make Your Own Rice Dumplings

1. Place opposite ends of two bamboo leaves together.
2. Fold leaves to form a cone.
3. Put one tablespoonful of rice into the cone and add 3 tablespoonsful of filling. Top up with one more tablespoonful of rice.
4. fold over leaves to cover the top.
5. Press stuffed leaves into pyramid shape.
6. Fold top piece of leaf to cover the top surface and fold remaining part to the side.
7. Use string to tie around the dumpling securely.
8. Cut away any long leaf edges.
9. Submerge the dumpling in boiling water containing pandan leaves and a little salt and cook for 1.5 to 2 hours.

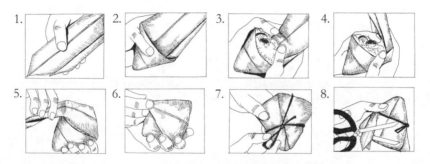

Dexterity-Imploring Day

The seventh day of the seventh lunar month is the Chinese Valentine's Day. It is also known as the Weaving Maid Festival and Daughter's Festival. This festival is closely tied to the love story about the weaving maid and the cowherd.

On the eve of the seventh day of the seventh month, the Cowherd Star (Altair) would be seen in the northeastern region in the sky, and opposite it in the northwest would be the Weaving Maid Star (Vega).

Seventh evening of the seventh month
On this night, young ladies would pray to the Weaving Maid and the Cowherd. The womenfolk in ancient times would thread a seven-holed needle. Being able to accomplish it quickly meant that one had deft hands. The womenfolk would also capture spiders and place one inside a box. They would open the box the next day, and if the cobwebs inside were dense, it would mean they had gained in dexterity.

The story of the Cowherd and the Weaving Maid
The Weaving Maid was the Queen Mother's daughter. She came to earth one day and met the Cowherd. They fell in love and were married, and had a son and a daughter. When the Queen Mother took the Weaving Maid back to heaven. the Cowherd gave chase but was stopped by the Milky Way. The magpies in the sky then formed a bridge for them. The Queen Mother finally agreed to let them meet each other on the eve of the seventh day of the seventh lunar month on the Magpie Bridge.

Zhong Yuan Festival

In olden times, the 15th of the first month, the seventh month and the 10th month were known as the Three Yuan. Tradition has it that during the seventh month, the gates of hell are opened and hungry ghosts are released to wander on the earth.

Originally, Zhong Yuan Festival was a day for the remembrance of ancestors. After Buddhism was introduced to China, the festival took on a Buddhist flavour and became known as *Yu Lan Pen Jie*. *Yu Lan Pen* has long been thought to be the Chinese transliteration of the Sanskrit term *ullambana*, meaning 'to be suspended in suffering' while *pen* in Chinese is a container for offerings. According to legend, this festival originated with the attempt of Mulian (Maudgalyayana, one of the Buddha's disciples) to save his mother.

As Chinese who are overseas may not be able to tend the tombs of their ancestors during the Clear Brightness Festival, they put extra effort in observing the rites for this festival.

Maudgalyayana's mother had died and fallen into hell, where she had to compete with hungry ghosts for food. Maudgalyayana had the power of clairvoyance and could see her plight. He tried to send her food, but when it reached his mother's hands, it would burst into flames. The Buddha taught him to make offerings of food to placate the other ghosts so that they would not snatch food from her.

Mid-Autumn Festival

Worshipping the Moon

During the early years of the Qin rule, the Chinese already had the practice of praying to the sun in spring and to the moon in autumn. The Mid-Autumn Festival is derived from the tradition of worshipping the moon. The forefathers believed that the harvest depended on the Moon Goddess. Without her showers of rain and constant changes to reflect the seasons, it would be impossible to have a bumper harvest of the five grains. Thus, the rites and rituals for moon worship were usually on a grand scale.

In ancient times, people believed that the sun was yang and the moon was yin. Hence, the deity that lived in the moon had to be a female fairy (the yin sex). The tale of Chang-e flying to the moon has been circulated since the Han Dynasty and she has been associated with the moon ever since.

The legend of Chang-e

Long ago, 10 suns appeared in the sky at once, causing much suffering to the people. The divine archer Hou Yi shot down nine of them and was banished to earth with his wife Chang-e to live as mortals. Later, Hou Yi acquired an elixir of immortality, but as he had changed for the worse after living on earth, Chang-e drank the elixir and flew to the moon alone.

Mooncakes

Mooncakes are round, symbolising reunion and completeness. Therefore, eating sweet mooncakes during the Mid-Autumn Festival represents the family's togetherness and living in sweet harmony.

Legend has it that mooncakes originated towards the end of the Song Dynasty, when the Mongols invaded China. The common people suffered under their rule and hence planned to revolt. To keep their plans from being discovered, they hid messages in round cakes which were sent to every family.

On the 15th night of the eighth month, the people rose up in revolt and killed the Mongol invaders as they slept. Mooncakes are eaten on this day every year to commemorate this event. The round cakes of the past have since evolved into the present-day mooncakes with fillings.

Make Your Own Mooncakes

Ingredients:
Snowskin flour 500g, sugar powder 100g, colouring, vanilla essence, lotus paste, red bean paste or custard 50g, salted half egg-yolk, mineral water.

Equipment:
Rolling pin and cake mould.

Method:
1. Mix the flour and sugar with some mineral water.
2. Add a few drops of vanilla essence and colouring.
3. Cut the dough into a few pieces and roll each piece into a thin circular shaped piece.
4. Combine the salted egg with some lotus paste / red bean paste / custard to make the filling.
5. Place some filling onto the rolled dough.
6. Seal the edges, place into the mould and press hard.
7. Knock the mould on a table and the mooncake will slide out.
8. Put the mooncakes into the chiller.

Chong Yang Festival

The ninth month is when the chrysanthemums blossom, and the ninth day of the ninth month is called Chong Yang Festival. It is also called Chong Jiu (Double Nine). In ancient times, on this day, people would climb hills to view the scenery. Everybody would drink chrysanthemum wine and pluck dogwood leaves and fruit. They would fill a red silk gauze with dogwood leaves and tie it to their arms. This was said to help prevent calamities.

In fact, during late autumn, the weather is dry and the vegetation starts to wither. It is easy for illnesses to spread, especially in places where there are a lot of people. Hence, climbing hills is not only a pleasurable activity, it can also help people to avoid pestilence. Dogwood and chrysanthemum have been used by people since ancient times for their medicinal properties as dogwood is said to be good for preventing pestilence, while chrysanthemum is used to treat a great variety of ailments and promotes longevity.

Thoughts of my brothers in Shandong on the ninth day of the ninth month

A stranger in a foreign place, thinking of home on festive days.
I know my brothers have hiked up the distant hills, carrying dogwood — without me.

~ Wang Wei, Tang Dynasty poet

Dong Zhi (Winter Solstice Festival)

Many people think that Dong Zhi means 'the arrival of winter'. In fact what Dong Zhi means is that after this day the sunshine will decline. In the northern hemisphere, the day is the shortest during Dong Zhi. In the southern hemisphere, it is the reverse.

During the Lunar New Year, everybody would visit one another. In olden times, during Dong Zhi, the people would do the same. Some people would offer incense at dawn and some businesses would take a break on that day. People would feast and the atmosphere was just like the New Year.

In China, because the onset of winter was cold and medical science was not advanced back then, many people froze to death at this time of the year. As a result, on this day, people would gather together to eat *tangyuan* as it is symbolic of family unity and harmony.

Solar Festivals

The Winter Solstice is one of the 24 Chinese solar festivals. The ancient Chinese divided the year into 24 solar terms based on the movements of the sun and moon, climatic changes and natural phenomena in agriculture and horticulture. The 24 solar terms are actually the 24 different positions of the earth in relation to the sun as it revolves around the latter. These are the 24 solar terms: Beginning of Spring, Rain Water, Waking of Insects, Spring Equinox, Clear Brightness, Grain Rain, Beginning of Summer, Lesser Fullness of Grain, Grain Beard, Summer Solstice, Lesser Heat, Greater Heat, Beginning of Autumn, End of Heat, White Dew, Autumn Equinox, Cold Dew, Frost's Descent, Beginning of Winter, Lesser Snow, Greater Snow, Winter Solstice, Lesser Cold and Greater Cold.

Tangyuan

"Every home will make *tangyuan* as the next morning will be the Winter Solstice." *Tangyuan* is a must-have during the Winter Solstice. They come in either red or white. There is a popular saying that goes, "If you do not partake of a golden (red) *tangyuan* and a silver (white) *tangyuan*, you will not grow a year older." Eating the *tangyuan* means one has grown a year older. *Tangyuan* must be swallowed in pairs for good luck. For a married person, if two *tangyuan* are left in the bowl, the person will have all wishes come true. If a single person has one *tangyuan* left, the person will have a smooth-sailing year.

Let's make Sesame *Tangyuan*

Ingredients:

Dough: glutinous flour, water.

Filling: sugar to taste, sesame paste, crushed walnuts, sesame seeds, wheat flour and lard.

Method:

1. Mix the sugar, sesame paste, crushed walnuts, sesame seeds, wheat flour and lard. Roll it and cut it into small square pieces.
2. Add cold water to the glutinous flour to form a dough. Pinch a small piece of dough off and wrap it around the filling. Roll it into a ball.
3. Add the balls (*tangyuan*) into water boiling at low heat. When the *tangyuan* floats to the surface, it is ready to serve.

SOCIAL ETIQUETTE

The Chinese are naturally hospitable and China has been called 'the country of etiquette'. In daily social dealings, etiquette is a must. In olden times, there were more social courtesies, and males and females even had different rules to follow.

Different types of bows

Kowtow
This was a show of deep respect for the monarch.

Bowing with knees on the ground
This was used between peers, or to ask a big favour of another party.

Good-fortune curtsy
Women in the old days would curtsy with their hands clasped at the right waist to show respect. As they bowed, they would wish the other party "good fortune".

Wishing good health (woman)
Women put both their hands on their knees, which were both touching the ground, and bow.

Wishing good health (man)
This was to show respect for the elders. One knee touched the ground while the other leg was bent.

A bow with hands clasped
Clasp your hands to show acknowledgement. This is done in non-official functions when you're with people you know well.

A deep bow with hands clasped
Clasp your hands, raise them high up then down. This is a show of great respect.

Bow
Keep your legs together and your hands at the side. Bend your body to show respect.

Receiving Guests

Offering tea

It is customary to offer a cup of tea to your guest. Whatever your social class, whether you are at a function, at work, at home, on a trip or in any other situation, tea is served whenever you entertain a guest.

When the host offers tea, he should do so with both hands to show respect. The cup should be three-quarters full, not filled to the brim. The guest then accepts the tea with both hands and takes a few sips, whether he's thirsty or not. This is to show respect and appreciation.

Accepting gifts

When a guest comes for a visit, he will usually bring with him a gift. The host should thank him and accept it graciously. The guest will be embarrassed if his gift is not accepted. Never open the gift before the guest as this is considered extremely rude.

Seeing the guest off

When the guest leaves, ask him to stay a while longer. Or invite him to visit again. The host should stand up and see him to the door.

When seeing him out, watch him go until he is some distance away. Never turn your back as soon as you have said goodbye as this is rude.

Giving Gifts

When attending a celebratory dinner, the gifts for the hosts are usually foodstuffs, fruit, fabric, cash, handicrafts or items for everyday use.

If you receive a gift from a guest, the gift you give him in future must be of greater value than his. It is rude not to return his kindness.

Offer gifts in pairs. An even number symbolises good luck and a good ending. However, do not give paired gifts to someone who is ill, as you may be wishing him "Misfortune doubled"!

In some places, it is taboo to use these articles as gifts:

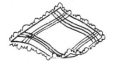

Handkerchief
It connotes parting with a person forever.

Scissors
Scissors connote the severing of ties.

Umbrella
To give an umbrella signifies a breakup.

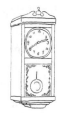

Flowers
Avoid giving jasmine or plum blossoms to businessmen. The former sounds exactly like *moli* 没利 (business losses) while the latter sounds like *mei* 霉 (bad luck).

Clock
It is taboo to give a clock as a birthday gift. 'Giving a clock' *(songzhong* 送钟) sounds like 'burying one's parent' (送终).

Red packets
In olden days, red was associated with life. As such, the Chinese revere the colour red. They use red paper to wrap things up as a sign of celebration and to ward off evil. Red packets are given away at weddings and birthdays, and also during the Lunar New Year.

Chinese Banquet Etiquette

Etiquette is very important when throwing a banquet. The basic practices followed today have been handed down from ancient times.

The first step is to issue an invitation card which is to express respect to the guest.

The table arrangement is centred around the main table. Guests are carefully ushered to the available tables. The first and second tables are usually reserved for the host and important guests. When there are many tables, table numbers are given. It is proper etiquette to wait to be seated by the host.

When assigning seats, guests are seated based on their seniority, status, kinship or wealth. This is the most complicated and important part of a banquet. A table usually seats eight, and the seating arrangements would differ between eras and regions. In all, the order of seats should *shang zuo zun dong* (respect both the left and the right), with the guest of honour facing the main door.

When taking their seats, modesty dictates that guests should offer one another the better seats. Hence, it is imperative for the important tables to be filled first before allowing the rest to take their seats.

Chopsticks are used at Chinese banquets, and there are some rules governing their use.
- Chopsticks must be neatly aligned in pairs.
- Don't hit an empty bowl with chopsticks.
- Don't plant chopsticks upright in the rice.
- Don't reach over someone else to pick up food.
- Don't waver indecisively with your chopsticks over the table.

Lunar New Year

To the Chinese, the Lunar New Year is the most auspicious and joyous of all festivals.

Left: Selecting Spring Festival couplets or scrolls. *Below:* The dragon dance is staged in hopes of a smooth and bountiful year ahead. In earlier times, it was used to pray for favourable weather in order to obtain good harvests.

Placing an inverted *fu* (prosperity) around the house symbolises that good fortune has arrived.

The God of Wealth is never neglected during the Lunar New Year.

Photos courtesy of Singapore Federation of Chinese Clan Associations, Yuan Magazine.

Dragon Boat Festival

In Singapore, the Dragon Boat Festival is usually celebrated by eating rice dumplings and participating in dragon boat races. Displaying calamus, drinking Xionghuang wine and wearing fragrant pouches are quite rare.

Right: The door is decorated with calamus and Chinese mugwort.
Below: Wrapping rice dumplings.

Top: A child chooses a fragrant pouch.
Left: Tracing the character *wang* (king) on the forehead of a child.

Dragon boat racing is now an international sporting event.

Photos courtesy of Singapore Federation of Chinese Clan Associations, Yuan Magazine.

Food

To the Chinese, eating is a very important part of life.

Mobile hawkers carrying
their wares.

Street stalls selling all sorts of food.

Besides rice, noodles are another staple of the Chinese people.

The Performing Arts

Fan dance.

Playing the diabolo.

Chinese music.

Chinese acrobatics.

Photos of dance, Chinese music, Chinese acrobatics courtesy of Singapore Federation of Chinese Clan Associations, Yuan Magazine; photo of diabolo courtesy of Feng Ge.

Chinese Opera

In Chinese opera, costumes are extremely colourful while the make-up is unique. Chinese opera attracts many fans with its "singing, reciting, action and fighting".

Chou (the villain or comic character).

Chou and his entourage.

Dan (the female character).

Sheng (the male character).

Photos courtesy of Singapore Federation of Chinese Clan Associations, Yuan Magazine.

Paper Cutting

The subject matter for Chinese paper-cutting art is extremely diverse. It can range from flowers, insects, birds and fish to virtually any image that is considered propitious.

Clay Figurines

Adorable clay figurines are loved by the young and old. It is an art form that is appreciated by both refined and popular tastes.

Bronzeware

China is one of the first countries to produce bronzeware.
The patterns on bronzeware have simple and classical lines.

Photos show replicas of ancient bronzeware.
From top (left to right): wine vessel *jue*, food container,
folding wine vessel *zhegong*, cauldon *li*, wine vessel Boge *you*, dragon-bell (chime).

Tang Dynasty Tri-coloured Glazed Pottery

A type of three-colour pottery painted with yellow, green and white dyes, the tri-coloured glazed pottery of Tang (*tangsancai*) specialised in horse figurines.

Photos show replicas of Tang Dynasty tri-coloured glazed pottery.

Other Handicrafts

Painted porcelain.

Blue-and-white porcelain.

Porcelain headrests.

Cloisonné enamel.

Snuff bottles.

Photo of snuff bottles courtesy of Yong Gallery; photo of blue-and-white porcelain courtesy of S.I. Wood Carver; other photos on this page courtesy of Bao Yuan Trading Pte Ltd.

Dough figurines.

Dough figurine
(Lord Guan Gong).

Wood carving
(Goddess of Mercy).

The common people view the tiger as a god-like creature with powers to ward off evil. Hence, shoes and hats bearing the tiger head motif were put on children for protection. This was to ensure their safe development.

Qipao or Cheongsam

The *qipao* is the traditional costume for Chinese women. It is so elegant that even non-Chinese women like to wear it!

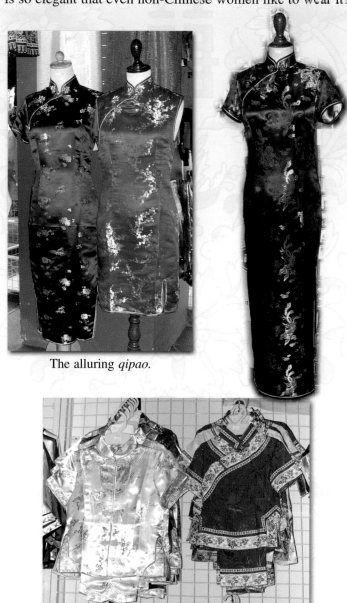

The alluring *qipao*.

Adorable Chinese-style costumes for children.

Photos courtesy of Chin Hing Emporium.

Calligraphy and the Four Treasures of the Study

The writing brush, ink stick, ink slab and paper are the four treasures of the study. They are indispensable in Chinese calligraphy.

Seals.

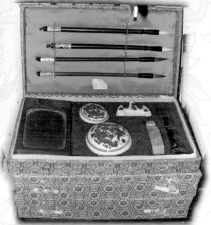

A calligraphy set with ink, brushes, inkstone and seal.

Works of calligraphy. On the right are the rarely seen oracle bone inscriptions.

Photos courtesy of Yong Gallery.

Religions

Chinese temples are where charitable
believers go to for spiritual guidance.

Photos courtesy of Thian Hock Keng Temple located at 137, Telok Ayer Street.

Thousand-armed Goddess of Mercy.

Mazu is the goddess that
protects seafarers.

The Town God is the protector
of town dwellers.

Left: The Warrior God, Lord Guan Gong. *Right:* Literary God, Confucius.
These are idolised and worshipped by many people.

Chinese Tea

There are many varieties of Chinese tea. Some are packed in tins, some in a round ball, some flattened and some come in a block.

Teapots are not only used to make tea, they are appreciated as ornaments too!

Photos courtesy of D' Art Station.

FAMILY

'All things go well when the family is harmonious' is an axiom of most Chinese families. Children and grandchildren must obey their elders and parents.

When the family is harmonious, the members will be blessed within and outside of the home. Philosophers say that 'when the family is together, the country is governed well, and peace comes to all'.

The ancient character for *jia* 家 (home)

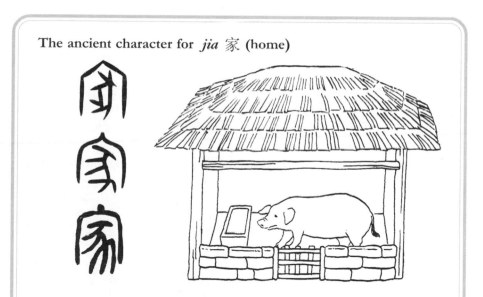

The character for home, *jia*, is a pig under a roof. The early Chinese were nomadic hunters. After they learnt to domesticate animals, they settled down in fixed areas. The domesticated animals were reared in the homes and thus the word was formed.

Family

Patriarchy

The traditional Chinese household runs along patriarchal lines. The father — or the grandfather, if he was still alive — is usually the head of the family. Only if the father and grandfather were both dead would the household be headed by the grandmother or mother. The head of the household wields absolute power and makes all the decisions for the family. The other family members have to listen to their instructions and obey their elders.

Extended families

Hence, in the past, China had many households with four, five and even nine generations living together. These huge households were actually made up of related smaller family units. They either shared the same father, grandfather or great-grandfather. There were usually more than a hundred people in the family. People in the past believed that it was good to have such a large extended family living under the same roof as it meant the family was flourishing and harmonious.

Today, it is rare to see such a huge family. Most households today comprise only the immediate family members with parents and children, or have no more than three generations, including the grandparents.

Family culture

The family culture refers to a family's regulations and living practices. This was extremely important in olden times as no matter how much power the family had, its standing in society would suffer if the family culture was poor. To maintain a proper family culture, a feudal household used domestic discipline and produced its own domestic teaching materials.

Domestic discipline

Each family member must abide by the law of the family. If the rules are broken, the offender must be punished accordingly. Incorrigible members would be disowned by the family and asked to leave the household.

Domestic teachings

Many teachings have been passed down through the generations, for example, *Administering the Household by Zhuzi* and *Domestic Teachings by Yan*. Descendants are indoctrinated in these teachings so that they will be good citizens and treat people with respect. Such teachings are still applicable today

> **The Chinese code of success**
> One should repair the house before it rains, and one should not start digging a well only when one feels thirsty.
>
> Do not keep in mind a favour you have bestowed on someone else, but do not forget to repay a favour you have received.

Upbringing

Traditional Chinese families place great emphasis on the development of moral character and proper behaviour. If a child has not been educated in these, it is considered the parents' failing. Chinese parents hate to hear that their child 'has no upbringing'.

Family courtesies

Traditional Chinese families place tremendous weight on respect towards elders and the seniority system. Family members must abide by a set of courtesies.

For example, children must be filial towards their parents and consult them in all matters, great or small. The children should greet their parents every morning and tuck their parents in at night. When eating, elders should start first.

The parents should be awe-inspiring but kind. Fathers usually feel great love for their children but hide it in their heart; hence, even in today's family units, we often see strict fathers and amiable mothers. Between brothers, the elder must love and teach the younger brother. The younger brother must view the elder sibling like a father and listen to him with respect.

Filial piety

Filial piety has always been of utmost importance among the Chinese. Confucius regarded filial piety and brotherly love as basic qualities in Man. With these two virtues, not only will the family be peaceful, society will also see less upheavals.

Mourning

In ancient times, mourning for one's dead parents was a very important task. The mourning period lasted for three years, during which time the mourner should not sing, dance, marry, or consume good food and wine.

Respecting the teacher

In ancient China, filial piety extended to elders and teachers. The Chinese call their teachers *Shifu* (Master-Father), and believed that a person who teaches you for a day, becomes your father for life. The status of the teacher was close to that of the father.

Terms of address

In the Chinese culture, seniority and relationships are very important, and this is reflected in the many terms of address used for relatives. In English, for example, the siblings of parents are simply called 'uncle' and 'aunt', their children 'cousins', while those related by marriage are termed 'in-laws'. In contrast, the Chinese distinguish each relation by relative age and generation, gender, and even whether

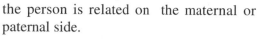

the person is related on the maternal or paternal side.

What all these considerations mean is, depending on the size of your extended family and the variety of relationships it contains, you may have to remember as many as 50 or more different titles, one for each relative!

Family relations

The 'nine generations' are the great-great-grandfather, great-grandfather, grandfather, father, son, grandson, great-grandson and great-great-grandson. This means nine generations with the same family name.

In ancient times, if somebody committed a heinous crime, he could implicate

his nine generations and get his entire family executed.

The 'three clans' include the father's clan, mother's clan and wife's clan.

The 'six relations' refer to the father, mother, elder brother, younger brother, wife and children. It could also mean one's relatives in general.

Relationship Chart: Maternal

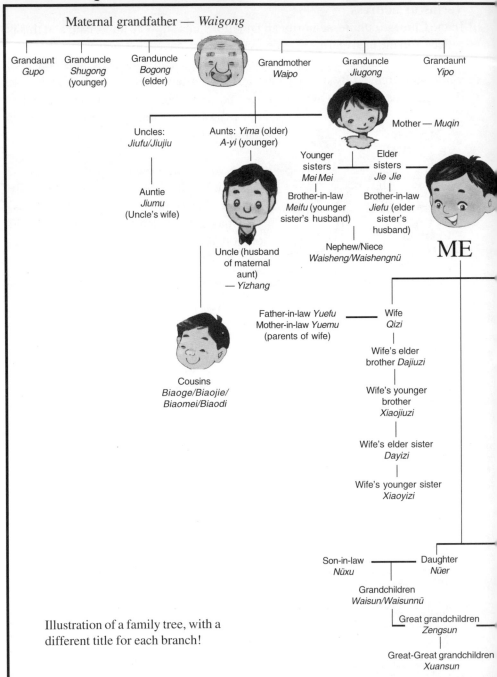

Maternal grandfather — *Waigong*

Grandaunt
Gupo

Granduncle
Shugong
(younger)

Granduncle
Bogong
(elder)

Grandmother
Waipo

Granduncle
Jiugong

Grandaunt
Yipo

Uncles:
Jiufu/Jiujiu

Aunts: *Yima* (older)
A-yi (younger)

Mother — *Muqin*

Auntie
Jiumu
(Uncle's wife)

Younger
sisters
Mei Mei

Elder
sisters
Jie Jie

Brother-in-law
Meifu (younger
sister's husband)

Brother-in-law
Jiefu (elder
sister's
husband)

Uncle (husband
of maternal
aunt)
— *Yizhang*

Nephew/Niece
Waisheng/Waishengnü

ME

Father-in-law *Yuefu*
Mother-in-law *Yuemu*
(parents of wife)

Wife
Qizi

Cousins
*Biaoge/Biaojie/
Biaomei/Biaodi*

Wife's elder
brother *Dajiuzi*

Wife's younger
brother
Xiaojiuzi

Wife's elder sister
Dayizi

Wife's younger sister
Xiaoyizi

Son-in-law
Nüxu

Daughter
Nüer

Grandchildren
Waisun/Waisunnü

Great grandchildren
Zengsun

Great-Great grandchildren
Xuansun

Illustration of a family tree, with a
different title for each branch!

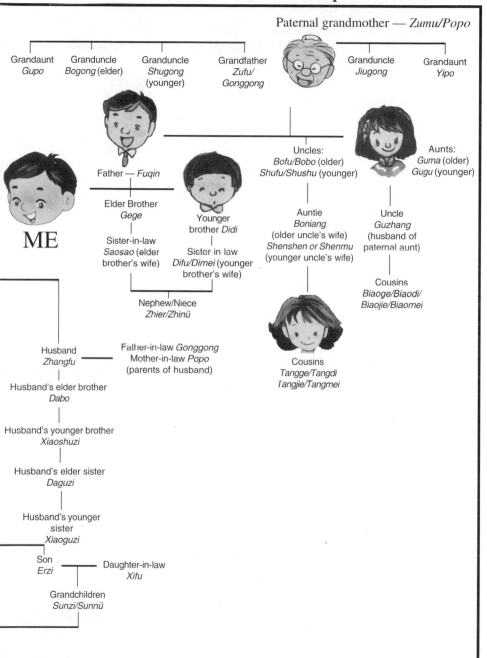

Paternal grandmother — *Zumu/Popo*

Grandaunt
Gupo

Granduncle
Bogong (elder)

Granduncle
Shugong
(younger)

Grandfather
Zufu/
Gonggong

Granduncle
Jiugong

Grandaunt
Yipo

Father — *Fuqin*

Uncles:
Bofu/Bobo (older)
Shufu/Shushu (younger)

Aunts:
Guma (older)
Gugu (younger)

ME

Elder Brother
Gege

Sister-in-law
Saosao (elder
brother's wife)

Younger
brother *Didi*

Sister-in-law
Difu/Dimei (younger
brother's wife)

Auntie
Boniang
(older uncle's wife)
Shenshen or Shenmu
(younger uncle's wife)

Uncle
Guzhang
(husband of
paternal aunt)

Cousins
Biaoge/Biaodi/
Biaojie/Biaomei

Nephew/Niece
Zhier/Zhinü

Husband
Zhangfu

Father-in-law *Gonggong*
Mother-in-law *Popo*
(parents of husband)

Cousins
Tangge/Tangdi
Tangjie/Tangmei

Husband's elder brother
Dabo

Husband's younger brother
Xiaoshuzi

Husband's elder sister
Daguzi

Husband's younger
sister
Xiaoguzi

Son
Erzi

Daughter-in-law
Xifu

Grandchildren
Sunzi/Sunnü

Boys are better than girls

In feudal China, boys were favoured over girls. Apart from special circumstances, such as a female head of the household or a daughter-in-law from an influential family, most women had no place in the family. A common Chinese saying goes, 'Obey the father at home, obey the husband when married, and obey the son when widowed.'

Traditional Chinese culture valued chastity highly. All women had to abide by the code of chastity. If her husband was dead, the woman would remain chaste in his memory. For women who were outstanding in preserving their chastity, the government would even commend their efforts and build chastity memorial archways for them.

Bringing glory to the family

The Chinese hold the patriarchal clan (members with the same male lineage) and the family's reputation in great esteem. Each member sees himself as an important part of this clan or household. Hence, honour to the family is also honour to oneself.

Likewise, the family's disgrace is also one's disgrace. To bring honour to one's clan and family is the primary dream of most traditional Chinese people.

LITERATURE

China's major forms of literature include poetry, essays, novels and operas. Each dynasty had its own literary contributions. For example, the Tang Dynasty was a golden era for poetry, the Song Dynasty was an age of *ci* song poetry, the Yuan Dynasty was famous for its dramas, and the Four Great Literary Classics appeared during the Ming and Qing Dynasties.

These remarkably varied works have created an extremely rich and bountiful literary treasure trove.

The origins of Chinese literature can be traced to China's ancient past. At that time, tools were relatively simple and people had to exert tremendous energy in labour. In the course of hard labour, people naturally developed a rhythmic grunt to synchronise with the work. This sound was dubbed 'work song'.

The content of work songs gradually became filled with meaning, and developed into rhythmic poems and songs. Later on, these songs were sung when people danced or worshipped the gods. Unfortunately, the songs were not recorded as the written word had not been created yet.

Below is a famous work song called 'Land Tilling Song' said to have been handed down from the time of the legendary emperors Yao and Shun:

I labour when the sun rises,
I rest when the sun sets.
Dig a well for water to drink,
Till the land for crops to eat.
What can kings do for me?

Myths and Legends

Mythology existed long before the advent of writing. Passed down the generations through the oral tradition, only a fraction of these stories have been recorded in writing and preserved in classical documents. These beautiful myths influenced and provided great inspiration to later literature.

Genesis in Chinese Mythology:

Pan Gu opens the sky

A long time ago, heaven and earth were joined in the form of a large egg, in which Pan Gu slept. One day, he awoke and broke the eggshell in half. The lighter half rose to become heaven while the heavier portion sank and became earth. Afraid that heaven and earth would come together again, Pan Gu braced up heaven with his arms and stamped on the earth with his feet. Tens of thousands of years later, the heaven became higher and higher, while the earth became thicker. The two halves became separate entities. Exhausted, Pan Gu died. After his death, his left eye became the sun and the right eye, the moon. His body was transformed into mountains and his blood into rivers. His hair turned into flowers, grass and trees while his perspiration became raindrops. His whole body was given to the great earth.

Nüwa creates humans

After the creation of heaven and earth, earth was a bleak and desolate place as there were no humans yet. The Goddess Nüwa came and moulded several figurines of mud in her image. These mud figurines ran everywhere; some headed east or west, and the rest went to either the north or south. These were the first human beings.

Pre-Qin Literature

The Book of Songs

The Book of Songs is China's first compilation of poems, with 305 poems from the Early Western Zhou period to the middle of the Spring and Autumn Period, a period of 500 years, and is said to have been compiled by Confucius.

The Book of Songs may be categorised into local folk songs, court songs of King Zhou's period, and songs of praise used for sacrifices.

The Songs of Chu

The Songs of Chu are mainly Qu Yuan's works. It has both long and short verses, and uses many meaningless sounds.

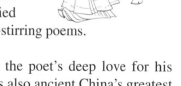

China's first poet, Qu Yuan was King Huai's trusted official, but the king believed malicious rumours and sent him into exile. During his long exile, he worried over the country and people, writing many heart-stirring poems.

Qu Yuan's masterpiece, 'The Lament', evokes the poet's deep love for his country with beautiful and emotional verses. It is also ancient China's greatest Romantic work.

> **Qu Yuan's 'Li Sao' (The Lament)**
> *My way lies remote and so far; I shall go up and down on my long search aye.*

Essays

Shang Shu (*The Book of History*) was the first collection of historical documents in China. *Zhuo Zhuan* (*Spring and Autumn with Commentary by Zuo Qiuming*) and *Zhan Guo Ce* (*Anecdotes of the Warring States*) were representative works from the pre-Qin era.

Pre-Qin philosophers like Zhuangzi, Mencius, Mozi and Han Feizi also used many interesting analogies and stories to get their point across.

Han Dynasty Literature

Han Fu (rhymed prose of the Han Dynasty)
This is a literary form that appeared during the Han Dynasty. Representative authors include Sima Xiangru and Jia Yi.

Records of the Historian
The most outstanding piece of work on history was written by Sima Qian. *The Records of the Historian* kept accounts from the legendary Huangdi to Han Wudi, spanning a period of over 3,000 years and covering economic, cultural and artistic developments as well as many important historical events and figures.

Book of Han
The Book of Han by Ban Gu of the Eastern Han Dynasty is China's first recording of dynastic history, though it covers only the Western Han period.

Yue Fu (Musical Institution)
Han Dynasty folk songs were collected, sorted and maintained by a musical institution for performance in the palace and during events. Hence, they are popularly known as Yue Fu folk songs. 'Kong que dong nan fei' (Wife of Jiao Chongqing) is a representative work from Yue Fu and is the longest narrative poem in China, depicting the tragedy of a young couple.

Nineteen Ancient Poems
A group of short poems by an unknown author, they had five characters in each line and were usually about human relationships, social ties and love.

Jian'an literature
In 196 AD, on the orders of Emperor Xian of Han, Cao Cao moved the capital to Xuchang and renamed the era Jian'an. As the situation then was in chaos, the poems of the period had a unique heroic but mournful tone, known as the Jian'an Style. Representatives of this style include Cao Cao and his two sons, Cao Pi and Cao Zhi, jointly known as the Three Caos.

Cai Yan, the lady poet
Cai Yan (Cai Wenji) was an outstanding poetess of the Jian'an Period. Her poems often described people's grief and sufferings.

Literature from the Wei, Jin, Southern and Northern Dynasties

Seven Sages of Bamboo Forest
Ruan Ji, Ji Kang, Shan Tao, Wang Rong, Xiang Xiu, Liu Ling and Ruan Xian were free-spirited poets of the Wei (Three Kingdoms) Period, who expressed their frustration and unhappiness through their poetry. Ruan Ji is the most highly regarded among them.

Tao Yuanming — A pastoral poet
Tao Yuanming of the Easten Jin Dynasty is the founder of pastoral poetry. His poems were beautiful and simple. Tao Yuanming did not care for an official post, preferring to till the land and admire chrysanthemums. His famous saying, "I will not bend my will for five *dou* of grain", became the catchphrase of those who didn't hanker after fame and fortune.

Tao Yuanming's 'Drinking Wine', 5 of 20
I built my cottage among the habitations of men,
And yet there is no clamour of carriages and horses.
You ask: "Sir, how can this be done?"
A heart that is distant creates its own solitude.
I pluck chrysanthemums under the eastern hedge,
Then gaze afar towards the southern hills.
The mountain air is fresh at the dusk of day;
The flying birds in flocks return.
In these things there lies a deep meaning;
I want to tell it, but have forgotten the words.

Landscape poets

Xie Lingyun was the first to write landscape poetry. Another outstanding poet of this genre was Xie Tiao. The popularity of their poetry can be seen in a saying of the time: 'Three days without reading Xie poems makes one feel as if one has bad breath.'

Folk songs from the Southern and Northern Dynasties

Folk songs from the Southern Dynasty usually revolve around love and romance. Those from the Northern Dynasty are frank and unconstrained, with a wide range of subjects from scenery to the brutalities of war. Among them, 'Song of Mulan' tells of how Hua Mulan dressed up as a boy to take her father's place as a soldier, while 'Song of Chi Le' describes the vast northern steppes.

Song of Chi Le (Northern Dynasty)

On the prairie vast, under the azure sky, when the wind sweeps past, the grass stoops low and the flocks and herd appear.

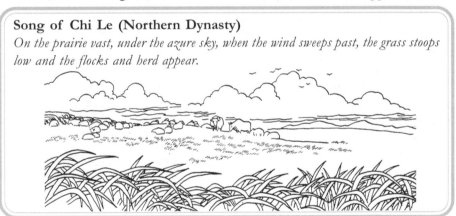

Short stories

These appeared during the Northern and Southern Dynasties. They can be classified into *zhiguai* and *zhiren*. *Zhiguai* fiction centres on ghosts and monsters. *Sou Shen Ji* (*Records of Spirits*) by Gan Bao is a representative work from this genre. *Zhiren* fiction focuses on records of people's remarks and anecdotes. *Shi Shuo Xin Yu* (*New Anecdotes of Social Talk*) by Liu Yiqing is an example.

Poetry critique

Wen Xin Diao Long (*Carving a Dragon in the Heart of Literature)* is a classic that critiques Chinese literature. Zhong Rong's *Shi Pin* (*Poetry*) is a book that critiques poetry and prose.

Tang Dynasty Literature

Chinese literature flourished during the Tang Dynasty. There are more than 50,000 Tang poems still in circulation today. Tang poetry can be divided into early Tang, prosperous Tang, mid-Tang and late Tang periods.

Tang poems are written in two styles — ancient and contemporary. The ancient style has no limitation to the number of lines or the tonal patterns. The contemporary style has the *lüshi* and *jueju*. Both follow a strict structure, with a set number of lines and tonal patterns.

> ### 300 Tang Poems
> "Those who read Tang poems often enough know how to recite them if not write them." *300 Tang Poems* is a collection of the most well distributed and influential poems from the Tang Poetry archives. It was compiled and edited by Hengtang Tuishi of the Qing Dynasty.

Early Tang poets

Four major poets of the early Tang period are Lu Zhaolin, Luo Binwang, Wang Bo and Yang Jiong, of which Luo Binwang and Wang Bo are best known. Wang Bo's 'Teng Wang Ge Xu' (Pavilion of Prince Teng) is the most influential.

Chen Zi'ang opposed the extravagant writing style of the Six Dynasties and advocated wholesome topics for poems, revolutionising Tang poetry.

Wang Wei is representative of the landscape and pastoral school. His forte lay in describing the natural landscape and its sounds. He wrote many acclaimed poems which Su Shi, a great literary figure of the Song Dynasty, complimented as being akin to paintings.

> ### Wang Wei's 'Song of Wei City'
> *In Wei City morning rain has drenched the light dust;*
> *Green, green the young leaves of the willows beside the inn.*
> *Let me persuade you — empty one more wine-cup:*
> *There are no friends where you are going west of Yang Pass!*

Meng Haoran

Meng Haoran was the first major Tang poet for landscape and pastoral poetry. His poems were known as 'fresh poems' for their fresh, natural, flowing lines.

'Chun Xiao' (A Spring Morning) by Meng Haoran
I awake light-hearted this morning of spring,
Everywhere round me the singing of birds
But now I remember the night, the storm,
And I wonder how many blossoms were broken.

Wang Zhihuan's 'Deng Guan Que Lou' (Ascending Stork Pavilion) was the most celebrated and influential poem of its genre.

'Deng Guan Que Lou' (Ascending Stork Pavilion) by Wang Zhihuan
The sun sets behind the mountain, the Yellow River flows into the sea.
If you want to look afar, you must get one level higher.

Frontier poems

Frontier poems depict the scenery and landscape of the border and express the feelings of those stationed at such forts. Gao Shi and Cen Can were the most famous Tang frontier poets besides Wang Changling and Wang Han.

'Chu Sai' (To the Frontier) by Wang Changling
A bright moon of the Qin, a pass of the Han.
Men yet to return from the 10,000-mile expedition.
If only the Flying General of the Dragon City were here.
No Hu cavalry shall pass the Yinshan Mountains.

Li Bai

Li Bai is considered the ultimate Tang poet. A lover of wine, he was known as the poet who wrote 100 poems while drinking. He was also known as the Poetry Deity. His poems were full of imagination and feeling, with a very strong distinctive character. His 'A Tranquil Night' is known by all.

Before my bed a pool of light,
Is it hoarfrost upon the ground?
Eyes raised, I see the moon so bright;
Head bent, in homesickness I'm drowned.

Du Fu

Du Fu is hailed as the Sage of Poetry and enjoys the same prestige and honour as Li Bai. Du Fu travelled widely and, troubled by the sufferings of the common people he saw, these concerns colour his poetry. As his poems reflected his times, he became known as the Historian Poet.

"The vermilion gates smack of the stench of wine and flesh, the roads are covered in frozen bones."
Du Fu penned this famous line after seeing how the rich people squandered their money in drinking and merry-making, and how the poor suffered from the cold and hunger.

Mid-Tang poets

Meng Jiao's 'You Zi Yin' (A Traveller's Woes) is an ode to his mother that has been passed down the generations.

The threads in a kind mother's hand; A gown for her son bound for far-off lands,
Sewn stitch by stitch before he leaves; For fear his return be delayed.
Such kindness as young grass receives; From the warm sun can't be repaid.

Bai Juyi

Bai Juyi's famous 'The Everlasting Regret' is about the love story between Emperor Xuanzong and Yang Guifei.

> *"On high, we'd be two lovebirds flying wing to wing;*
> *On earth, two trees with branches twined from spring to spring."*
> *"The boundless sky and endless earth may pass away,*
> *But this vow unfulfilled will be regretted for aye."*

Late Tang poets

Poetry from the late Tang period was often melancholic. The outstanding poets of this era were Li Shangyin and Du Mu, popularly known as 'Li and Du, Junior' as they shared surnames with Li Bai and Du Fu.

Prose

For classical prose writing, Han Yu believed that literature and morality should be joined. He advocated the revival of Confucianism and pre-Qin traditions while opposing the extravagant prose style of the Six Dynasties, and called for the adoption of a simple and rustic style instead. Han Yu was also among the Eight Great Prose Writers of the Tang and Song Dynasties, which included Liu Zongyuan, Ouyang Xiu, Zeng Gong, Wang Anshi, Su Shi, Su Xun and Su Zhe.

Fictive Chronicles (*Chuanqi*)

Such stories covered a wide range of topical subjects. They had complex plots and fresh, vivid characters. Representative works are Bai Xingjian's *Chronicle of Li Wa* and Yuan Zhen's *Story of Yingying*.

A poet emperor — Li Yu

At the end of the Tang Dynasty, China saw the rise of the Five Dynasties and 10 States. Li Yu was the last emperor of the Southern Tang. When Song destroyed Southern Tang, Li Yu was made a prisoner of war. His poems are full of yearning for the mountains and rivers of his country as well as his grief and sorrow.

Quotes from Li Yu

"The regrets of life are as long as the river runs east."
"May I ask how deep your sorrow is? It's as deep as the eastern river."

Poetry of the Song Dynasty

Song Dynasty literature

The Song Dynasty was the time of *Ci* poetry. *Ci* poems could have lines of varying lengths and were originally song lyrics. Each *Ci* follows a tune such as 'Pu Sa Man' and 'Cai Sang Zi', which had a set form for the number of lines or characters as well as pitch and tonal patterns.

Su Shi

Su Shi, also known as Su Dongpo, is considered the greatest of the Song poets. Su Shi's father, Su Xun, and his brother Su Che were also literary figures, and together they were known as the Three Sus.

His works were vigorous and sprightly, belonging to the free school of writing. His masterpiece 'Missing the Slave on the Bridge', about Zhou Yu of the Three Kingdoms, tells how Zhou Yu foiled the Cao army's plans.

> **Famous quotes from Su Shi's poems**
>
> *"Men know joy and sorrow, parting and reunion;*
> *The moon lacks lustre, brightly shines; is full, is less.*
> *Perfection was never easy to come by."*
> *"Though miles apart, could men but live forever*
> *Dreaming they shared this moonlight endlessly!"*
> *"The Yangtze flows east, Washing away, A thousand ages of great men."*

Liu Yong

Liu Yong was adept at music and contributed much to the development of *Ci* poetry. Before him, most *Ci* poems were shorter. Liu Yong composed many tunes with slow rhythms to allow more characters in the *Ci*. His *Ci* poems were so widespread it was said that wherever there was a well, there would also be someone singing Liu's *Ci* poems.

> **Liu Yong's famous words**
>
> *A tearful ending comes to those with many feelings.*

Wang Anshi

Wang Anshi was a statesman who combined politics with literature. He believed that knowledge should be used appropriately and used literature as a tool to achieve his political aspirations.

> **Wang Anshi's celebrated lines**
> *Now that spring breezes have made the south bank green,*
> *when will the bright moon see me on my way home?*

Patriotic poets

In 1127, the Jins attacked and invaded Bianjing of the Song Dynasty. Song Gaozong went southwards and built a small imperial court in Jiankang. Following the fall of Northern Song, the Southern Song Dynasty was born. Many patriotic poets appeared during this period. Among the more famous ones are Lu You and Xin Qiji. 'A River Red' by the famous general Yue Fei is also acclaimed.

> **Famous lines by Wen Tianxiang**
> *Death befalls all, I would rather leave behind a crimson heart*
> *to shine in the tablets of bamboo!*

Li Qingzhao

The greatest female Chinese poet, Li Qingzhao's poems were filled with the sorrow of parting and the changing times. Her verses were beautiful and elegant, yet moving. 'Sheng Sheng Man' is considered her masterpiece.

> **Famous lines by Li Qingzhao**
> Li Qingzhao gives very vivid portraits of anxiety, for example:
> *This feeling cannot be dispelled; Just now it leaves my brow; Only to come into my heart.*
> *I fear that my small grasshopper boat at Twin Stream, cannot be moved, many sorrows.*
> *Do not tell me not to be held spellbound, when the curtain flutters in the west wind, I am*
> *thinner than the yellow chrysanthemum.*
> *This sequence, how can the word 'sad' sum it all up?*

Ouyang Xiu

Ouyang Xiu is one of China's most renowned Song Dynasty poets and historians. He was an advocate of the neo-classical style of writing where simple language was used in poems. His most celebrated work is 'Zui Weng Ting Ji' (Record of the Old Tippler's Pavilion).

Ouyang Xiu's famous lines

The old tippler's heart is not in the cup, but on the landscape. He drinks not to get drunk but rather to give expression to nature and so transcend the fleeting ups and downs of politics and the world of men.

Fan Zhongyan

Fan Zhongyan was a famous litterateur and a leader of the political reform movement in the Northern Song Dynasty. The few works he left behind were mostly about the society of the time.

"Be the first to show concern for the people and the last to enjoy."

This line comes from his masterpiece, 'Yue Yang Lou Ji' (The Yueyang Pavilion), which shows his concern about his country and fellow men.

Zhou Dunyi

Zhou Dunyi's 'Ai Lian Shuo' (Love of the Lotus) is a famous poem about the nobility of the lotus that remains pure despite being born out of the mud.

Song Dynasty *huaben*

During the Song Dynasty, the empire was prosperous, there was a marketplace culture and different art forms appeared. Among these, story-telling became a popular art form and was known as *shuohua* or talking. These performers used *huaben* or story-telling scripts when relating their stories to the audience. With some improvements and editing, the scripts become storybooks or what is known as *baihua xiaoshuo* (plain language novels).

There are four types of Song Dynasty story-telling scripts. The two major types are *xiaoshuo* (novel), which are short and focus on current social conditions, and *jiangshi* (historical novel) or *pinghua,* which is drawn from history and is so long that each story would take several sessions to complete.

Yuan Dynasty Literature

The dramas and lyric songs of the Yuan Dynasty are known as *yuanqu*. Guan Hanqing, Ma Zhiyuan, Zheng Guangzu and Bai Pu are known collectively as the Four Great Dramatists of the Yuan Dynasty.

Guan Hanqing

The most prolific and outstanding dramatist, Guan Hanqing can be said to be China's answer to William Shakespeare. Guan wrote a total of 60 dramas, among which *Dou E Yuan* (*Injustice to Lady Dou the Widow*), *Jiu Feng Chen* (*Salvation of the Abducted*), *Wang Jiang Ting* (*River View Pavilion*), and *Bai Yue Ting* (*Moon Worship Pavilion*) are considered his masterpieces.

Ma Zhiyuan

His masterpieces are *Han Gong Qiu* (*Autumn in Han Palace*), about Wang Zhaojun being sent to the frontier, and the song 'Tian Jing Sha, Qiu Si' (Ode to the Clear Sky, Thoughts in Autumn), for which he is called Ancestor of Autumn.

> **Ode to the Clear Sky, Thoughts in Autumn**
> *A withered vine still clings to the old tree in which the crows nest;*
> *A little bridge lies across the stream which flows past houses;*
> *A lanky horse trudges along the ancient road, and the west wind blows.*
> *The sun is settling down in the west,*
> *The remotest corner of the earth sees a stranger much distressed.*

Wang Shifu

Wang Shifu's internationally renowned masterpiece *Xi Xiang Ji* (*Romance of Western Bower*) has made famous its protagonists such as Hong Niang, Cui Yingying and Zhang Sheng. Matchmakers have come to be known by the name Hong Niang, after the character who brought Zhang and Cui together.

Ming Dynasty Literature

The novels of the Ming Dynasty had significant achievements with representative works such as *San Guo Yan Yi* (*Romance of the Three Kingdoms*), *Shui Hu Zhuan* (*The Water Margin*), *Xi You Ji* (*Journey to the West*) and *Jin Ping Mei* (*Golden Lotus*).

Romance of the Three Kingdoms, written by Luo Guanzhong, recounts the time of the separatist warlord regime in the late Han Dynasty, with Cao Cao, Liu Bei and Sun Quan as its protagonists. The story promoted the spirit of loyalty and righteousness, making it an integral part of the Chinese cultural tradition.

The Water Margin, written by Shi Naian, is about the rebellion during the late Northern Song Dynasty. The narrative tells of the tyrannical acts of corrupt officials, and how Song Jiang, Lin Chong, Wu Song and the others who comprised the 108 good men were forced up Mount Liang.

Journey to the West was written by Wu Cheng'en during the Ming Dynasty. It narrates the journey of a Tang monk to fetch Buddhist scriptures from India. The author added colour to the story with fantastic characters like Sun Wukong, Zhu Bajie and Sha Wujing to turn it into a mythological story.

Golden Lotus, written by Lan Ling Xiao Xiao Sheng, was the first novel to be written independently by Chinese literati. It was also the first to focus on family life, human relationships and social ties. The book tells the story of the philandering Ximen Qing and his three concubines.

The well-known novel *Feng Shen Yan Yi* (*Canonisation of the Gods*), edited by Xu Zhonglin, is a tale about gods and monsters set during the later Shang period when King Wu of Zhou was attempting to depose King Zhou of Shang.

The Three *Yans* and Two *Pais*
The Three *Yans*: *Yu Shi Ming Yan* (*Stories to Enlighten Men*), *Jing Shi Tong Yan* (*Stories to Warn Men*) and *Xing Shi Heng Yan* (*Stories to Awaken Men*) are three collections of short fiction selected and edited by Feng Menglong.

The Two *Pais* are *Chu Ke Pai An Jing Qi* (*Amazing Stories First Series*) and *Er Ke Pai An Jing Qi* (*Amazing Stories Second Series*), compiled by Ling Mengchu.

Chinese drama
Tang Xianzu was the most prolific dramatist of the Ming Dynasty.

His four works – *Zi Chai Ji* (*Tale of the Purple Hairpin*), *Mu Dan Ting* (*Peony Pavilion*), *Nanke Meng* (*Nanke Dream*), and *Handan Ji* (*Story of Handan City*) – are collectively known as *Lin Chuan Si Meng* (*The Four Dreams of Lin Chuan*).

Among these, *Peony Pavilion* is the most well-known and is critically acclaimed worldwide.

Qing Dynasty Literature

A Dream of Red Mansions was written by Cao Xueqin during the Qing Dynasty. The story revolves around four families serving the imperial court — the Jia household, the Wang household, the Shi household and the Xue household. It depicted the rise and fall of these four big households. The main theme is the romance between Jia Baoyu and Lin Daiyu.

A Dream of Red Mansions, **excerpt from 'Hao Le Ge'**
Everyone knows that gods are good, but cannot forget fame and fortune!
Where have all the soldiers gone? The land lies waste!
Everyone knows that gods are good, but cannot forget about money!
I lament that we have not much time left. I may be dead when we meet again!

The Scholars
Written by Wu Jingzi, *Ru Lin Wai Shi* (*The Scholars*) is a classic sardonic novel that attacks the imperial examination system and feudal ethics.

Four Great Condemnation Novels
Li Boyuan's *Guan Chang Xian Xing Ji* (*Exposure of the Official World*), Wu Yanren's *Er Shi Nian Mu Du Zhi Guai Xiang Zhuang* (*Strange Events of the Last Twenty Years*), Liu E's *Lao Can You Ji* (*Travels of Mr Derelict*) and Zeng Pu's *Nie Hai Hua* (*Flower in an Ocean of Sin*) are jointly known as the Four Great Condemnation Novels of the Late Qing Dynasty.

Strange Tales of Liaozhai

Written by Pu Songling, *Liaozhai Zhi Yi* (*Strange Tales of Liaozhai*) is China's most influential collection of short stories. The author used stories about ghosts, fox spirits, flower imps and fairies to satirise the social conditions of his time, mock human nature and praise true love. Many of the stories, such as 'Nie Xiaoqian', 'Laoshan Dao Shi' (Taoist Priest of Mount Lao) and 'Hua Pi' (The Painted Skin), have received widespread acclaim.

Ji Xiaolan

A collection of short fiction called *Yue Wei Cao Tang Bi Ji* (*Notes of Yuewei Hermitage*) by Ji Xiaolan (Ji Yun) is also a good representative of this era.

Opera

Hong Sheng and Kong Shangren were outstanding playwrights during this period. *Chang Sheng Dian* (*Palace of Eternal Youth*) by Hong Sheng is a love story about Emperor Xuanming of Tang and his beloved concubine Yang Guifei.

Tao Hua Shan (*Peach Blossom Fan*) by Kong Shangren is a historical drama about the love story between scholar Hou Fangyu and Li Xiangjun, a courtesan, with the prosperity and decline of the Ming Dynasty serving as a backdrop.

Zheng Banqiao

A poet, painter and calligrapher, Zheng Banqiao was one of the Eight Eccentrics of Yangzhou. He was acclaimed for the Three Incomparables (art, prose and calligraphy) and the Three Truths (true spirit, true sincerity and true humour).

Gu Wen Guan Zhi

Gu Wen Guan Zhi (*Best of Classical Prose Writing*) is a popular collection of Chinese prose writings from pre-Qin to the Ming and Qing Dynasties selected and edited by Wu Chucai and Wu Diaohou.

THE ARTS

Elegant Chinese music, graceful dance steps, unique operas, Chinese brush paintings and calligraphy are all splendid examples of Chinese art forms. Art is not just a performance, it has to be able to capture people's hearts. The ancient Zhou Dynasty placed much importance on music and had created large institutions to teach music and govern music matters. Art can soothe and stabilise emotions. It could be due to the calming effects of calligraphy that most calligraphers live to a ripe old age!

Confucius and music

Confucius was not just a great philosopher and educator. He was also an outstanding musician. He had such a great love for music that though he encountered many difficulties during his tour of the various states, he never stopped playing music.

When he heard the ancient song 'Shao' 韶 in the state of Qi, he was so mesmerised by it that he could go without meat for three months.

Confucius believed in the political and educational components of music. He emphasised the marriage of rituals and music, which he felt would help in changing established habits and social customs, and in maintaining law and order.

Confucius attached great importance to the moral integrity of music. He believed that music should be guided by moral values and was strongly opposed to the mere enjoyment of music. His ideal music was one that was not too self-indulgent and excessive in emotions.

Music

Music in religious rituals

Music was first closely linked to religious rituals. Musicians during that time were sorcerers. During the Zhou Dynasty, *liuyue* 六乐 was offered as a sacrifice to Heaven and Earth, the sun and the moon, mountains, rivers and forefathers.

Music and politics

Duke Zhou of the Zhou Dynasty created rituals and music, making music one of the two main pillars in maintaining order. At that time, music had heavy political undertones.

Officials from the emperor down to minor officials all had their own orchestras. The arrangement and number of musicians were based on the rank of the official.

The art of music

By the Wei, Jin, Northern and Southern Dynasties, music had become a purely artistic expression of thoughts and emotions. Thereafter, music developed in all directions into the variety that is available today.

Types of musical instruments

Chinese musical instruments have a history going back thousands of years. There are hundreds of instrument types, which can be classified into four categories – wind, bowed, plucked and percussion. Ancient Chinese musical instruments were made from metal, stone, earth, wood, calabash, leather, silk and bamboo, which are collectively known as the Eight Tones.

> ### *Guqin* 古琴
> The *guqin* is the king of ancient Chinese musical instruments. A highly versatile stringed instrument, it can produce a wide range of different tones, and has a resonant yet mellow timbre.
>

Dance

Dance is one of the oldest forms of art. China's primitive dances were derived from the expression of feelings towards certain things such as hunting, production, or love and affection. Primitive dances can be for entertaining the gods or for their own enjoyment. Dances that are meant to entertain the gods often involve praying

and rituals to reflect their religious beliefs, while dances for personal enjoyment include the hunting dance, celebratory dance and step dance.

Classical dance flourished during the Han Dynasty when the art form was highly regarded. There were dancers in the Han palaces as well as rich households. During the Three Kingdoms Period, popular dances include the long-sleeves dance, mixed couple dance, sword dance and sabre dance. The art form was further developed during the Tang Dynasty. The Rainbow-Feathered Dress Dance was the most renowned at that time. Dance was embraced by the common people during the Ming and Qing Dynasties, who invented dances such as the harvest dance, dragon dance, lion dance and the big-headed doll.

Folk songs

The many ethnic groups in China all have their distinctive folk songs. The northern songs are known for unconstrained forthrightness while those from southern China are appreciated for their lyrical beauty.

The Han people have the most number of folk songs, which can be classified into three types — the work song, mountain song and canzonet. Work songs are sung while working and are concise and uninhibited. Mountain songs, with high notes and free rhythms are sung when in the mountains or in daily life, and canzonets are sung for entertainment or during special occasions. The songs have regular rhythms and intricate melodies.

Beijing Opera

Beijing opera

The early Qing Dynasty saw a great development of a plethora of operas. In the middle of the Qing Dynasty, Hui and Han operas were brought into Beijing. They became immensely popular with the imperial family, nobles, officials and the commoners. The marriage of Hui and Han operas became known as the Beijing opera.

Beijing opera consists of singing, recital, gestures and fighting actions. The song-and-dance routine, the dazzling costumes, the stylised performance and colourful facial make-up were a huge draw.

Stylised action

Beijing opera recreates settings and props through the use of mimed gestures and actions. The stage has no real door, carriage, boat, mountain or horse; hence the actors will mime the action of opening a door, entering through the door, getting on a carriage, rowing a boat, climbing up a mountain and riding a horse.

For example, the hands showing the action of holding a rein means the actor is riding a horse, the act of opening a door means just that and walking round the stage in one circle means a long journey.

Chinese facial make-up is a unique part of Chinese opera. Chinese opera is based on these four character types:

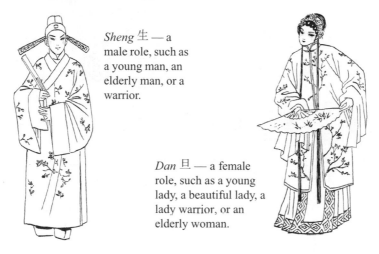

Sheng 生 — a male role, such as a young man, an elderly man, or a warrior.

Dan 旦 — a female role, such as a young lady, a beautiful lady, a lady warrior, or an elderly woman.

The make-up for *sheng* and *dan* roles should highlight the eyes and eyebrows and the application of rouge. This type of make-up is known as the *sumian* 素面 (plain face).

Jing 净 — also known as the painted face, used on a chivalrous and rugged male role.

Chou 丑 — also known as the little painted face, used on villainous or comic characters.

Jing and *chou* follow a standard way of make-up. It uses different colours and strokes to exaggerate the actors' features, either to beautify them or to make them ugly. They are used to show the personality of the character and to add a touch of drama to the role. This is the Chinese facial make-up that we are familiar with.

Various Kinds of Facial Designs

Three-part make-up (*sankuaiwa* 三块瓦)
It emphasises the forehead and cheeks. Used on heroes and warriors.

Worn-out face (*polian* 破脸)
Also called broken face or old face, the strokes, patterns and colours used on these faces are more complicated. They express the character's innermost feelings.

Beancurd face (*doufukuailian* 豆腐块脸)
A white square is drawn around the nose. It is the pattern used for a *chou* role.

White face (*fenbailian* 粉白脸)
White powder is applied all over the face. A black pencil is used to highlight the eyes, brows, nose and muscles. It is used on cunning characters.

The facial make-up follows a standard format. You are not allowed to change the style or look of a character. The colours are classified as primary, secondary, peripheral and complementary. No matter how complicated the make-up may be, there is always one main colour used to highlight the role's character.

The meaning behind the colours used in facial make-up:
Red — loyalty and courage
Yellow — cruelty and savagery
Golden yellow — gods and demons
White — evil
Blue — carelessness and impetuousness
Black — righteousness
Green — chivalry

Xiang Sheng

The comic dialogue *xiang sheng*
Comic dialogue is an artistic form based on 'talking, imitating, teasing and singing'. This art form only became a profession during the reign of Emperor Tongzhi of the Qing Dynasty, with a history of more than a hundred years. Despite this, in earlier times, comic dialogue can also be seen in entertainment acts such as *Feiyou*, *Baixi* (100 acts) and *Xiaohua* (jokes).

Comic dialogue can be divided into categories such as monologue (one person), cross-talk (between two people, one acting dumb and the other intelligent), and group dialogue (three or more people).

Comic dialogue relies heavily on 'talking', and gets its laughs through imitating the sounds, actions, and expressions of subjects. The performers can also copy other art forms with songs (singing) to 'tease' the audience. Comic dialogue can only be considered successful when it manages to obtain laughter from the audience.

Talking and singing arts
Also known as folk arts, the talking and singing arts depend on talking and singing. Other forms besides comic dialogue are story-telling, drum or clapper talk, and ballad singing. One person may take on many roles to perform the story.

Performers usually carry a couple of musical instruments (for drum talk and ballad singing), a paper fan (for story-telling), a set of bamboo pieces (for clapper talk) or nothing at all (comic dialogue).

Painting

Portraiture: The subject is a person. This is the earliest type of painting in China.

Bird-and-flower compositions: Flowers, grass, bamboo, stones, birds, animals, fish and insects are the main themes.

Landscape: Nature is the subject. It became another theme for painting during the Tang Dynasty. This form of painting developed most rapidly.

Techniques in Chinese painting

The techniques in Chinese painting may be classified into the following schools of styles: *gongbi* 工笔 (literally: fine brushwork), *xieyi* 写意 (literally: write ideas), or a combination of both.

Gongbi painting
The brushstrokes are neat and attention is given to details.

Xieyi painting
The brushstrokes are less well-defined. Emphasis is placed on the overall expression and the painting is subject to the whim of the individual painter.

Colour

In Chinese paintings, the ink is the dominant feature while colours are peripheral. Chinese painters classify the black ink into five 'colours': concentrated, thick, heavy, thin and light.

Black is considered a colour and more colours can be represented by varying the intensity.

White space

White spaces are often seen in Chinese painting. They are considered a part of the painting. They add life to the painting and give room for imagination.

Chinese painters now and then
- The Tang Sage of Art, Wu Daozi, specialised in painting Buddhist figures.
- Gu Qizhi of Eastern Jin paid special attention to the expression of the eyes and would not draw the eyes of a portrait subject until he had observed the subject for a few years.
- The Eight Eccentrics of Yangzhou were painters during the Qing Dynasty who focused on painting flowers and broke with tradition with their free expression. Zheng Xie (Zheng Banqiao) was the most famous of the eight and he specialised in painting orchids, bamboo and stones.
- Qibaishitou's prawns, Zhang Daqian's lotus and Xu Beihong's horse are the Three Supremes in the world of art in modern China.

Picture mounting

Chinese paintings are also mounted to add brilliance to them. A painting is not considered to have been completed until it is mounted, a requirement unique to Chinese paintings.

A blending of components

A Chinese painting is a marriage of poetry, calligraphy, seal and image. National artists often indicate the theme of the painting, the artist's name and the date of the painting. Sometimes, a poem or a prose extract is written next to the painting. These verses and lines complement and enrich the meaning behind the painting. Seals are also affixed to embellish or balance the painting.

Seals
Often used in calligraphy and painting, the seal was usually carved from special stones.
There are many types of seals, mainly used for personal names and pseudonyms, and some are even engraved with warnings or poetry!

Calligraphy

Chinese calligraphy has been hailed as word art, emotive line dance, soundless music and colourless drawing. Hence, calligraphy is also called the ink dance.

Types of writing styles
In calligraphy, there are various writing styles. Among them are the seal, official, regular, running and walking styles. Each style has its own unique characteristics.

Zhuanshu 篆书 **(seal style)**
During the Qin and Han Dynasties, Chinese characters were long and curved.

Lishu 隶书 **(official style)**
The characters were flat and blocky in form.

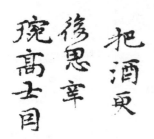

Kaishu 楷书 **(regular style)**
The most commonly seen style in calligraphy, the characters are squarish and regular, with full and beautiful strokes. This style reached its acme during the Tang Dynasty when the three great calligraphers of *kaishu* lived — Yan Zhenqing, Liu Gongquan and Ouyang Xun.

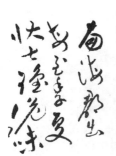

Caoshu 草书 **(running style)**
With expressive lines dancing with life and zest, this is a highly artistic form. Zhang Xu and Huai Su of the Tang Dynasty are best known for this style.

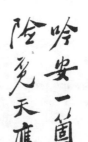

Xingshu 行书 **(walking style)**
A cross between the *kaishu* and the *caoshu*. This is the style used by Wang Xizhi of the Eastern Jin Dynasty, who was known as the Sage of Calligraphy.

Wei-Jin Dynasties — Wang Xizhi
Orchid Pavilion Preface
Considered to be the quintessential representative work of *xingshu*. It contains a total of 324 words, and each word has its own distinctive character.

The Sage of Calligraphy — Wang Xizhi

Wang Xizhi of the Eastern Jin Dynasty is considered the greatest calligrapher in Chinese history and hailed as the Sage of Calligraphy.

He is said to have spent 20 years practising calligraphy, and after every practice session, Wang Xizhi would wash his brush in the pond next to his house. As time passed, the water in the pond turned blackish. It later became known as the Ink Pond.

His son, Wang Xianzhi, was also a noted calligrapher, and they are known by later generations as the Two Wang calligraphers.

Four Treasures of the Study

In ancient times, brushes, ink, paper and inkstones were indispensable in writing and painting. Together, they were termed the Four Treasures of the Study.

Brush

The brush is a writing instrument that is peculiar to China, with a history of over 2,000 years. Brushes come in many varieties, and the brush tip can be made with hair from the rabbit, goat, horse, mouse, wolf, fox, gorilla, goose, duck, chicken, pig, or even a baby. The handle too can be made from precious or common materials, from ivory and jade to bamboo.

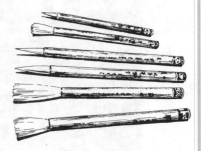

Ink

Where there is brush, there is ink. Originally, ink had to be ground and have water added to it before it could be used, but during the late Qing Dynasty, liquid ink was invented. Using this proved to be more convenient.

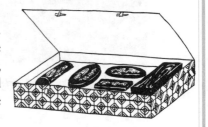

Paper

One of China's Four Great Inventions. During the Eastern Han Dynasty, a clever official by the name of Cai Lun innovated the process of paper production. He mixed together tree bark, hemp, cloth fragments and fish net to produce a fine white paper which was easier to write on.

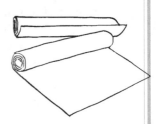

Inkstone

In China, the inkstone is used to grind pigments for writing or painting. It is also the only one of the Four Treasures that can be handed down as an heirloom. Inkstones can be stone, copper, ceramic or lacquerware.

CRAFTS

There are many different Chinese crafts, such as pottery, silk, embroidery, clay figurines, paper-cutting, and bronzeware. Most of these art forms have long histories behind them and unique ethnic styles. These extraordinary crafts showcase the intelligence and dexterity of the Chinese people.

Some of these crafts were originally articles for daily use. For example, pottery containers were used to hold food or store grain, bronzeware were usually food containers, wine vessels or weapons. Paper cuttings were used to adorn doors and windows. As they were exquisite, these items became a form of art.

Today, we throw away our umbrellas and mirrors when they wear out or become damaged without any hesitation. China has many beautiful waxed paper umbrellas, silk umbrellas and antique bronze mirrors that are in a different league from our usual umbrellas and mirrors. They are works of art collected by connoisseurs!

Waxed Paper Umbrella
Pictures of flowers, birds and scenery are hand-painted onto the surface of the umbrella. The surface is then varnished with a layer of tung oil to waterproof it.

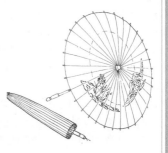

Silk Umbrella
Made of fine silk as thin as silk threads, the umbrella is supported by a bamboo frame and painted with scenes from nature. It is extremely light and handy.

Bronze Mirror
Bronze mirrors have intricate designs and patterns.

Ceramics

China is the native home of earthenware and porcelain. As China is well known throughout the world for its porcelain, which is also known as china, Europeans first got to know about the country because of its porcelain. Eventually, they decided to call the country which produced china China.

Porcelain

The making of earthenware paved the way for the discovery of porcelain by the Chinese. Different colours of porcelain developed over the centuries as people experimented with glazes. Later, people began to produce white and painted porcelain. Today, blue-and-white porcelain is the most recognisable variety, with glass and plastic dishes made to look like blue-and-white porcelain.

Tri-colour glazed pottery

Tri-colour glazed pottery made its appearance during the Tang Dynasty. Tri-colour glazed pottery is a kind of brightly coloured pottery that uses mainly yellow, green and white colours. Images of people, animals and everyday objects were commonly seen on tri-colour glazed pottery. Those with images of horses were the most common and most beautiful. Hence, they were very popular too. Tri-colour glazed pottery was mostly used as burial items. The emperors, royalty and nobles of the Tang Dynasty were buried with tri-colour glazed pottery.

Silk

China was the first country in the world to discover silk. For more than 6,000 years, the Chinese have been breeding silkworms to make silk from their cocoons. The ancient Greeks knew China as Seres, which meant the Silk Country. When silk was introduced into the Western world, the Westerners fell in love with the beautiful material, which was made into many different types of fabric.

The ancient Silk Road began at Chang'an (known as Xi'an today) and continued through Hexi, Xinjiang, Congling (known as the Bomier Highlands today), West Asia and finally Europe, covering a total distance of more than 7,000 km.

For a long time, the Silk Road remained ancient China's longest international trade route. It was a meeting point for Eastern and Western cultures and served as an important economic bridge. The name came about because silk enjoyed the highest trade volume and the greatest popularity along this route.

The founding of the Silk Road

During the Western Han Period, Emperor Hanwu sent Zhang Qian to the Western Region as an envoy. Zhang Qian was captured by the Huns and held captive for 10 years. In 119 BC, he made a second attempt. This time, he took with him more than 300 men and visited many places in the Western Region. He also took along many trade goods like silk, metal wares and lacquerware, and brought back the seeds of grapes, pomegranates, walnuts and carrots. Thereafter, merchants, peasants, monks and travellers followed in a ceaseless stream between the East and the West.

Embroidery

Chinese embroidery has enjoyed such great popularity that every region has its own unique style. Let us look at the four main types.

Suzhou embroidery
The picture is simple and the embroidery intricate. Favourite subjects depicted include cats, goldfish and white peacocks.

Hunan embroidery
The style is simple and the picture realistic. Lions and tigers are its most common subjects.

Guangdong embroidery
It is colourful and boasts many kinds of stitchwork. The traditional subjects are the phoenix heading towards the sun and two dragons playing with a pearl.

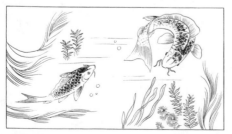

Sichuan embroidery
Pretty and vivid, its primary subjects are the hibiscus, carp, rooster and cockscomb flower.

Clay Modelling

Clay toys became very common in China at the start of the Tang Dynasty. It was a folk art that was suitable for both the young and the old. Even the emperor took a liking to them.

Wuxi, Hangzhou, Suzhou and Tianjin count among the more famous places for clay toys. Clay toys are not just limited to images of children. They also include opera figures, the God of Longevity, top scholars, animals and everyday objects. Very often, they expressed the people's wish for a good life.

Niren Zhang

Niren Zhang is a famous form of clay-modelling from Tianjin in northern China. Originating during the late Qing Dynasty, it has been passed down five generations to the present. The originator of Niren Zhang, Zhang Mingshan, had been adept at kneading clay into figurines since he was a child. It is said he would hide some clay in his sleeves whenever he went to watch operas. As he watched, he would knead his figurines, and before the show ended, he would have made vivid clay models of the characters. Niren Zhang has a wide repertoire that includes character caricature, folklore and mythical characters, etc.

Wuxi's clay figurines of little children

Wuxi is well-known for its clay figurines of little children. Emperor Qianlong travelled to Mount Huiquanshan on his Jiangnan tour and encountered a clay figurine master called Wang Chunlin. Qianlong ordered him to make five plates of clay children and bestowed on him beautiful gold plates and silks. From then

on, Wuxi's clay figurines of little children became widely known.

Paper Cutting

Paper cutting involves cutting holes out of paper to create beautiful works of art. This art form goes a long way back. Excavated ivory, bones and earthenware belonging to the New Stone Age were found to have carvings which seemed to be done with the method of paper cutting.

Themes for paper cuttings
There is no limit to the themes and subjects. Anything goes for paper cutting. Below are some examples of the more commonly seen images:

These express auspicious meanings like many offspring and celebration.

They can also be done in the form of flowers, grass, worms, birds, scenery and lanterns.

Some reflect scenes from life, such as weaving, fishing and cow herding.

Others depict scenes from folklore and history like Madam White Snake and Wu Song Killing the Tiger.

The Bronze Age

Bronzeworking was already highly advanced during the Shang Dynasty and the Zhou Dynasty. The bronzeware, strong and exquisite, was finely crafted.

Bronzeware was also used in everyday life in the form of food containers, wine vessels, musical instruments and weapons.

Besides being dignified, solid and beautiful, carved on the Shang bronze vessels were interesting patterns comprising of exaggerated, mystical and freakish emblems. There were also long inscriptions on the ancient bronze objects known as *jin wen* or *zhong ding wen*.

Made during the late Shang Dynasty, the 875 kg Simuwu rectangular cooking vessel is the largest bronzeware ever unearthed in the world.

Among the Warring States musical instruments that were unearthed, the set of large *bianzhong* chimes is the most valuable. The chimes can still produce beautiful music after being buried for more than 2,400 years.

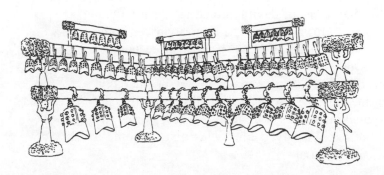

Others

Lacquerware

Lacquerware is an ancient and highly valuable art form with a history of over 7,000 years. Mixed with dyes, the sap from the lacquer tree produced lacquered objects with a smooth and shiny finish. The bright colours, pictures and designs painted on them make the objects attractive and eye-catching works of art.

Carving

Chinese carving covers a broad spectrum, and the main types include stone carving, jade carving, woodcarving, ivory carving and bamboo carving. However, even items like cowrie shells, cow horns, charcoal and coconut shells can be carved as well. The variety available is endless!

Cloisonné enamel

During the Jingtai reign of the Ming Dynasty, artisans discovered a deep blue glaze which made the most beautiful wares. Cloisonné enamel thus became known as Jingtai Blue (*jingtai lan* 景泰蓝). In ancient times, cloisonné enamel was reserved for royalty, and it was a symbol of power and status.

Wax-dyeing

Wax-dyeing is one of the traditional handmade floral printing art forms in China. The minority tribes in the southwestern region had already grasped the techniques of wax dyeing way back during the Qin to Han Period. To this day, wax-dyeing remains a very popular skill among these peoples. Wax dye is highly decorative and is favoured on dresses, wall pictures, accessories and table cloths. Wax-dyed cloth has also become a fashionable material.

Dress

Qipao or Cheongsam

If we had to select a dress to represent the Chinese woman, it would no doubt be the *qipao* or cheongsam!

Once the traditional costume of Manchurian women, the *qipao* was later adopted by Han women. It was said that Shanghainese schoolgirls were the first Han women to wear the *qipao*. Other women began to copy them, and it became an official national costume for women in 1929.

The *qipao* that Manchurian women wore during the late Qing period was loose and straight, with its length reaching the feet. Many design changes to areas such as the collar, sleeve, length, fabric colour and buttons were incorporated into the *qipao* during the 1930s, along with Western influences such as a more figure-hugging cut.

In the 1940s, the *qipao* got rid of its sleeves, shortened its length and reduced the height of its collar, making the dress more comfortable and convenient to wear.

Sleeveless *qipao*

The knee-length *qipao* with a narrow collar

Long sweeping *qipao* with short slits

The Chinese tunic suit or Zhongshan suit

The Zhongshan suit is one that depicts the characteristics of the Chinese nation. It was designed by Dr Sun Yat Sen, the man who toppled the Qing empire and set up the Republic of China.

During the Qing Dynasty, men had pigtails, donned skullcaps and wore a mandarin jacket over a long gown. After Dr Sun Yat Sen became the Provisional President of the Republic of China, he advocated cutting off the pigtails and wearing functional clothes.

Combining traditional Chinese and Western dress influences, he used the Cantonese daywear as a base, added a flipped collar over a straight collar, and converted the west's three inner pockets into four outer pockets.

Under Dr Sun's advocacy, the Zhongshan suit grew in popularity and has become a national costume.

The long gown and mandarin jacket of the Qing Dynasty

The Zhongshan Chinese suit

FOOD AND BEVERAGES

As the famous saying goes, 'people view food as heaven' (food is of utmost importance to people). To the Chinese, eating is a very important part of life. The ancient people of 2,000 years ago have already expressed this idea: 'Eat, drink, man, woman, herein lies the basic desires of humans' (*Records of Rites*) and 'Food and lust, this is nature' (*The Analects*). Today, when the Chinese meet, they would often greet one another with the query, "Have you eaten?" Not only do the Chinese love to eat, they love to cook too. Chinese cuisine is internationally renowned and there are Chinese restaurants everywhere.

Eating is also a social activity and the Chinese love to give dinner treats. Eating can help alleviate tension and break the ice. In addition, one can tell a person's behaviour from the way he eats. Hence, there is better understanding after a meal.

In Chinese society, 'eating' is a measure of the success of a government, as represented by the saying, 'The ruler views his subjects as king, the people view food as heaven.' Politicians also use 'eating' as a strategy. Whoever is able to feed the people will rule the people.

Features of Chinese Cuisine

To the Chinese, cooking is an art in itself. Chinese cuisine places emphasis on colour, aroma and flavour. Not only must a dish taste good, it must also appeal to the senses to be able to whet the appetite.

The many different cooking techniques

There are countless ways to cook the same ingredients, and each way of cooking imparts its own unique flavour to the food. You can steam, double-boil, stew, poach, sauté, braise, stir-fry, shallow-fry, deep fry and many more.

The eight main cuisines

Chinese cuisine can be divided into eight main regional branches:
- Sichuan, with characteristic rich and spicy dishes like Gongbao Diced Chicken;
- Shandong, which is particular in its selection of ingredients for dishes like Dezhou braised chicken;
- Suzhou, and its carefully presented steamed crucian carp;
- Guangdong, with distinctive sweet and crispy dishes like roast suckling pig;
- Fujian, famed for Buddha Jumps Over the Wall;
- Zhejiang, which emphasises fresh food and natural flavours, particularly seafood;
- Huizhou, which favours delicacies from the land and sea; and
- Hunan, which features rich foods with strong colours like cured meats.

Confucius once said: "Food can never be too refined, meat can never be sliced too thin."

This saying aptly shows that the pursuit of excellence is the essence of Chinese cuisine.

Health begins with a healthy diet

An ancient saying tells us that 'Health begins with a healthy diet.' Food was considered central to the preservation of health and the treatment of illness. During the Zhou Dynasty, there were 'food physicians', evidence that the earliest medical specialists were dieticians as well. These were the common opinions of ancient doctors in China regarding diet and healthy living.

Tonics

Besides their daily staples, the Chinese also like to use various herbal medicines to make tonic soups. Tonics are for everybody. There's a saying: 'If you're sick, the tonic will cure you; if you are not, it will strengthen your body.' A typical Chinese is nourished with tonics all his life. Students use it to energise themselves and to promote physical and mental growth. Women take it for one month after giving birth to hasten recuperation. Old folks also need the boost to maintain their aging body.

There's a popular saying among the people: one should eat like to nourish like. For example, one must eat pig's brain to nourish the brain; and pig's leg to nourish the leg.

Tea

Tea is consumed in over 100 countries and regions around the world. Among them, China is the earliest country to cultivate and drink tea. It is a popular beverage that is enjoyed by people from all social strata in China.

The discovery of tea

It is said that tea was discovered by the legendary ruler Shennong, who sampled various kinds of herbs in order to help his people differentiate poisonous from medicinal plants. One day, he collapsed under a tree after tasting some poisonous leaves. Fortunately, water droplets that happened to trickle down from the tree into his mouth revived him. The tree was a tea plant. From then on, people came to know about tea, and began using it as a medicine because of its detoxifying and other healthful effects. Because it's refreshing, thirst-quenching, fragrant and delicious, tea gradually became an everyday drink.

Lu Yu — the Tea Master

During the Tang Dynasty, there was an expert on tea — Lu Yu. He wrote *Tea Classic*, the world's first treatise on tea leaves. The book had detailed accounts on how to grow, prepare and drink tea, the varieties of tea, tea utensils, the effects of the quality of water used for brewing, as well as the customs of tea drinking. It had a far-reaching influence on the development of tea culture, elevating tea drinking into a specialised art.

Lu Yu, the Tea Master, was the patron saint of the tea trade. The owners of teahouses often decorated their desktops with porcelain statues of Lu Yu. When business was slow, the vendors would pour boiling water into the hole on top of the figurine's head, a ritual that was said to improve business.

The types of tea

Green tea	This is an unfermented leaf that gives a lovely jade green brew. Green tea is very popular now. Longjing tea and Biluochun tea are both green teas.
Black tea	A fermented leaf that draws well and produces a red beverage. Among the black teas, Qimen tea from Anhui is the most famous.
Oolong **tea**	A semi-fermented leaf. It's dryer and keeps very well. Wuyi Yan tea from Fujian is the best-known *oolong* tea.
Scented tea	This is a type of flavoured tea, made by mixing the leaves of black tea, green tea, and *oolong* tea with various flowers. The jasmine tea from Fujian is the most renowned.
Compressed Tea	They are compressed tea leaves, made by steaming and then compacting the tea leaves into various shapes. Pu'er tea from Yunnan and Tuo tea from Sichuan are the best compressed teas.

Brewing water

Making a good brew requires good water, as it is the water that brings out the bouquet of the tea leaves. Lu Yu made these conclusions on the quality of brewing water.

Mountain spring water is the best.

River water is second.

Well water is the worst.

Wine

Wine has a long history in China, with the first brew made as early as 5,000 years ago. The beverage is indispensable in everyday life and at social events, be it festive celebrations, gatherings with friends and relatives, and happy or sad occasions.

The First Wine
Legend has it that a long time ago, the goddess Yi Di fermented the first wine by wrapping rice in mulberry leaves, which she then offered to Emperor Da Yu.

Some also say that wine was first made by Du Kang during the Zhou Dynasty. One day, while herding his sheep, he discovered that the millet porridge he had left in a bamboo tube for half a month had turned into fragrant wine. The name 'Du Kang' thus became synonymous with wine.

The types of wine

Rice wine

An ancient type of liquor, rice wine is made from glutinous rice and has a low alcohol content. When this wine is ready, it must be kept in earthen jars, which are then sealed with clay and stored in cellars. It is usually stowed for three to five years, and sometimes ten to twenty years. That's why it's also called vintage wine. Famous rice wines include Shaoxin Jiafan, Huadiao, Zhuangyuanhong.

White spirit

Its alcoholic content is so high that it's inflammable, giving rise to its alternative name, *shaojiu* (burning spirit). It is made from starch, Chinese sorghum and corn. Well-known white spirits include Maotai from Guizhou, Old Cellar from Luzhou in Sichuan and Fen from Shanxi.

Grape wine

Grape wines have low alcohol content and thus are not strong intoxicants. Grape wines originated from the ancient Asian countries of Babylon and Assyria, and reached China through the Silk Road during the West Han Dynasty. The best wines are those from northern China, such as Yantai and China Red Wine.

Herbal liquor

Herbal liquor is made from herbs and medicine. A favourite among the elderly, it's ideal for maintaining good health and promoting longevity. There are many kinds of medicinal wine, such as those made from pepper, osmanthus flower, chrysanthemum, glutinous rehmannia, wolfberry, tuckahoe or sealwort.

Chopsticks

Chopsticks are distinctive Chinese utensils that have at least 5,000 years of history. Besides its role in dining, a pair of chopsticks also carries many connotations that made it a part of the Chinese culture.

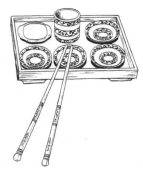

China is an agricultural society. Since the old days, grains like millet and husked rice cooked into rice or porridge have always been the staple food of the people. Using chopsticks to rake the rice or porridge is easier than using a spoon.

The development of chopsticks
The primitive forms of chopsticks were bamboo sticks and twigs. By chance, people found that they could use the sticks to pick up food, and modified them for use. In time, the sticks evolved into today's chopsticks.

Chinese started using chopsticks as early as 5,000 years ago. However, in the beginning, spoons were used more often, and chopsticks were only used to pick up pieces of food from the soup. It was not until the 14th century, during the Ming and Qing Dynasties, that chopsticks became popular.

Communal chopsticks
Emperor Gaozong of the Tang Dynasty always used two sets of chopsticks and spoons when he dined; one set for taking dishes from the plates, and the other for eating. This is because he was normally served more dishes than he could eat, and the leftovers were given to the maids and eunuchs. Emperor Gaozong used two sets of cutlery to preserve the hygiene of the food, and pioneered the use of communal chopsticks for common use.

MEDICINE AND SCIENCE

Chinese medicine and technology have thousands of years of history and contributed greatly to civilisation. With its unique diagnostic methods, Chinese medical treatment is world renowned. In addition, the four great Chinese inventions – gunpowder, paper-making, compass and printing technology – have made life more convenient.

Chinese scientific achievements are not limited to the four great inventions:

Seismograph

Zhang Heng of the Eastern Han Dynasty invented the world's first seismograph in 132 AD to measure earthquakes. The modern seismograph was only invented in the mid-19th century, more than 1,700 years later.

The decimal system

China was the first country to adopt the decimal system. In the bone-and-shell writings of the Shang Dynasty and inscriptions on bronzeware of the Eastern Zhou Dynasty, characters ranging from one to nine could be found, as well as characters representing the hundreds, thousands and ten thousands.

Iron and steel

Steel was invented during 4 BC in China. That was more than 1,000 years earlier than Europe. China was also the first to produce bronzeware.

Coal

China was the first country to mine and exploit coal.

Horticulture

Grafting was already widely used in China back in the sixth century to improve the shape, colour and quality of fruit and flowering plants.

Over 2,000 years ago, the Chinese were already using greenhouses to cultivate vegetables, more than 1,000 years ahead of the Europeans.

The Mystical Chinese Medicine

It integrates the yin-yang, five elements and the concept of man and nature as one entity in Chinese philosophy to develop a unique theory and system.

The Four Diagnoses

Chinese medical practice has no use for the stethoscope or other scientific equipment for the diagnosis of illnesses. Instead, it relies on the Four Diagnoses: observation, olfaction, interrogation and taking of the pulse.

Chinese medicine

Chinese medicine makes use of herbs, animals and minerals. Herbs make up a large part of Chinese medicine and are also the most widely used of the three groups. That is why Chinese medicine is also known as herbal prescriptions.

Compendium of Materia Medica

Li Shizhen, a physician during the Ming Dynasty, wrote the *Compendium of Materia Medica*, which lists 1,892 types of medicinal herbs and 11,096 prescriptions. A great medical classic, it has since been translated into many languages in many countries.

Acupuncture

Acupuncture uses needles and moxibustion to stimulate various acupoints. This method of treatment aims to treat the afflicted body part by balancing the yin and yang.

In acupuncture, needles are inserted into the acupoints through the skin.

In moxibustion, a piece of moxa is ignited to scorch the acupoint.

Massage

Massage uses hands to push, press, pinch or rub the body to stimulate blood circulation, increase the skin's resistance level and regulate the nervous system.

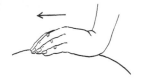

The Yellow Emperor's Internal Classic

Compiled during the Warring States Period, the *Yellow Emperor's Internal Classic* contains many medical anecdotes and theories in ancient China. This treasure of Chinese medicine is categorised into *Suwen* and *Lingqu*.

Bian Que

A famous physician during the Warring States Period, Bian Que introduced the Four Diagnoses. He was the first physician to diagnose illnesses by taking the patient's pulse.

Hua Tuo

Hua Tuo of the Eastern Han Dynasty pioneered anaesthesia, putting his patients under general anaesthesia for surgery on the abdomen.

Zhang Zhongjing

This Eastern Han Dynasty physician's famous work, *A Discourse on Colds and Various Ailments*, earned him the accolade of Ancestor of Prescriptions and Ancestor of Medicine.

Sun Simiao

This famous physician from the Sui Dynasty wrote many well-known books such as *Emergency Prescriptions* and *Preventive Prescriptions*. He was known as the King of Herbs.

Medical ethics

Medical ethics is a longstanding tradition in China. In addition to medical skills, a doctor must also possess a upright and moral character. There has been no lack of such benevolent doctors in Chinese history, and these men are still highly regarded in the medical field to this day.

Qin Feng, a Han Dynasty physician, treated his patients for free, asking only that they plant an apricot tree on the mountain where he lived. After many years, the apricot trees grew into a forest, and Qin Feng became known as the Benevolent Physician of Apricot Woods. 'Life among the apricot woods' and 'the apricots give life' became terms of praise for compassionate doctors.

The Four Great Inventions

Compass

The earliest of the four great Chinese inventions was the compass. More than 2,000 years ago, magnetic rocks were used in China to determine north-south directions. It was the forerunner to the compass.

The invention of the compass boosted the development of the nautical industry. Prior to this, seafarers had to observe the positions of the sun, moon and the stars to ascertain their direction. With the compass, more detailed navigation cartographs could be drawn. Sea navigation paved the way to greater interaction with the outside world.

The compass spread to the Arab world in the 12th century, and Europe in the 13th century. Its contribution to human civilisation cannot be underestimated.

The art of paper-making

During the Western Han Dynasty, there was a paper made of hemp, rags and old fishing net. Owing to its coarse texture, it was difficult to write on and never became popular.

During the Eastern Han Dynasty, Cai Lun, a court official, improved on the techniques of his predecessors to produce a paper that was finer, whiter and easier to write on. That spearheaded the popular use of paper and promotion of the Chinese culture.

The Chinese art of paper-making was introduced to Korea and Vietnam in the fourth century, Japan and the Arab world in the seventh century, and Europe and Africa in the 12th century, thus catalysing the development of human civilisation.

The art of printing

Ancient Chinese printing can be divided into block and movable-type printing.

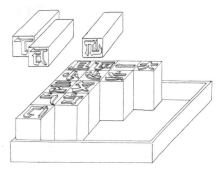

During the Northen Song Dynasty (1041 – 1048 AD), Bi Sheng, a craftsman at a book factory in Hangzhou, invented the movable-type method of printing. He carved characters on regular clay blocks, which he then fired. During the printing process, he would arrange the blocks in a metal holder and brush ink over them before stamping them on the paper. Afterwards, the characters could be rearranged to print different books, so the characters needn't be carved again, saving much time and effort. Any wrong characters could also be amended easily. This greatly increased the efficiency and volume of printing.

This method of printing spread to Korea, Japan, Vietnam and several other countries. It was only in the 15th century that Europe came up with its own movable-type system of printing, 400 years after Bi Sheng's invention.

Gunpowder

Gunpowder is created by mixing sulphur, saltpetre and charcoal in the correct proportions. Sulphur, nitre and charcoal were in fact medicinal compounds used in miracle pill formulas. Gunpowder was discovered during experiments to create such pills.

Gunpowder was first used in the military to manufacture explosives. Rockets, cannons and mines were first invented by China. Gunpowder was also used to manufacture firecrackers and fireworks, which the Chinese like to use to create a lively atmosphere on festive occasions.

In the 8th and 9th centuries, gunpowder was introduced to the Arab world. Europeans later learnt about gunpowder through their wars against the Arabs, providing a great impetus to weapons development in Europe.

Architecture

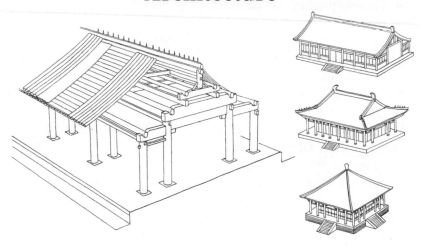

Ancient Chinese architecture used wood as the primary building material. Wooden pillars and beams formed the frame which bore the weight of the house. Walls only served to partition the house into various rooms. The sturdy wooden frame was able to withstand earthquakes.

Joinings
The wooden pillars and beams were securely joined using tenons and mortises, without the need for a single nail. This technique was discovered more than 7,000 years ago.

Support brackets
These support brackets extending from each pillar gave support to the beams and roof, strengthening the structure. The upward-curving eaves that were the product of this feature were not only decorative, but also resulted in a better-ventilated and brighter house. This technique first appeared 2,000 years ago.

Embellishment
Ancient Chinese roofs were often embellished with auspicious creatures to ward off evil and seek protection.

Various Types of Buildings

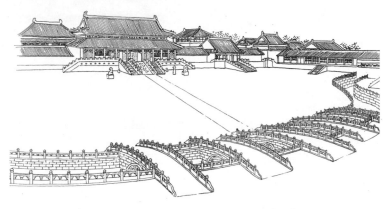

Palace: The dwelling place of ancient emperors and princes. The architecture is grandiose. The world-famous Forbidden City is made up of dozens of palaces and courtyards.

Temple: The place where ancient Chinese conducted prayer ceremonies and rites. The famous Beijing Temple of Heaven was used during the Ming and Qing Dynasties to offer prayers to heaven and prayers for a good harvest.

Residential houses: The common folks lived in these residential houses which came in all shapes and sizes, depending on the region. *Siheyuan* is the most representative of residential houses in Beijing. It is made of individual houses in the north, south, east and west wings. These houses are connected by walls and together, they form a quadrangle. The square compound forms the Chinese character for mouth (*kou*).

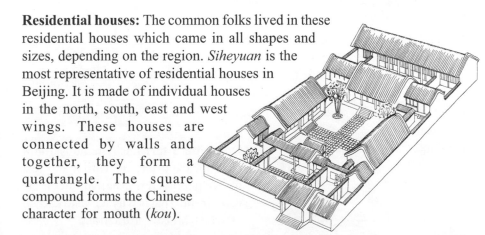

Garden: Ancient Chinese gardens are large and boast of mountain, lakes, flowers and trees. Pavilions complete the picturesque scenery of every Chinese garden. Gardens in Suzhou are the most famous.

Pavilion: These are built by the road or in gardens to offer shade and respite for the people.

Loft: Buildings with two storeys or more are known as lofts. They come in quadrangle, hexagonal or octagonal shapes. The buildings have open windows all around them and are usually built on highlands.

Terrace: It is a tall and flat building which facilitates a panoramic view.

Pagoda: It is built by Buddhists and ranges from five to 13 storeys high.

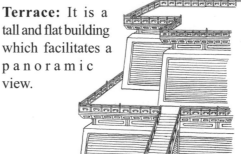

House on a terrace: The house built on a terrace offers recreation and rest for the people. It is usually built on the waterfront. That is why it is also known as water house on a terrace.

GAMES AND MARTIAL ARTS

The games that we play today such as chess, soccer, shuttlecock kicking and the swing have long historical origins. The Chinese also have other lesser known games such as Chinese rings and the seven-part puzzle which require skill and imagination. These games are good for developing mental agility.

The Chinese like to play chess, and here is some interesting chess jargon.

Cannon on the heels of the horse
The horse is one square away from the enemy's general or commander-in-chief on the same line, thus immobilising the latter. The cannon is then placed behind the horse and checkmates the opponent by leaping over the horse. This refers to a move that comes too late.

Offering a toast with two cups
A pair of cannons is used to attack the opponent's elephant in the rear.

Seeing Buddha home
The soldiers are used to force the opponent's general or commander-in-chief back to the starting point to clinch victory.

Deity showing the way
An opening move that allows one party to test the enemy's strategy by using soldiers to create an opening for the horse.

Weiqi (Go)

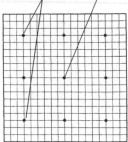

Xingwei *Tianyuan*

Weiqi, also known by its Japanese name Go, is a traditional Chinese chess game. It is said that *weiqi* was invented by Emperor Yao to train his son, Danzhu. *Weiqi* had already gained popularity during the Warring States Period.

Weiqi was introduced into Japan during the Later Tang Dynasty and was quickly incorporated into Japanese culture. In the 19th century, *weiqi* was introduced to Europe, and has since become a bridge for international cultural exchanges. Various countries hold regular *weiqi* competitions and seminars.

The ancient people called *weiqi shoutan* 手谈 (chatting with hands) or *zuoyin* 坐隐 (having a chat while seated together). Though the players do not converse, the seeds on the chess board express both parties' strategies and emotions.

Xiangqi

Xiangqi is a traditional Chinese chess game with a chessboard and 32 pieces.

The board consists of nine vertical and 10 horizontal lines, and the pieces are played on the intersections. There is a clear middle section on the board called the river, and four squares marked with a cross called the Ninth Palace.

Towards the end of the Tang Dynasty, the cannonball was invented and incorporated into *xiangqi*.

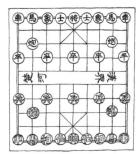

Xiangqi underwent a major revamp during the Northern Song Dynasty. The layout of the chessboard, the names of the pawns and the rules of the game were reinvented, establishing *xiangqi* as we know it today.

After the rules of the game and the chessboard were established, copper or wooden discs with characters printed on them gradually replaced the original three-dimensional pieces.

Chessboard and pawns for *xiangqi*

Other Games

Kite-flying

Kites were already flying in the skies of China about 2,000 years ago. They might have been the earliest flying invention. During the seventh and eighth centuries, kite-flying was introduced into Japan, Korea, Southeast Asia, Saudi Arabia, and finally Europe and America.

Legend has it a well-known artisan named Lu Ban invented the first kite, making it out of bamboo. During the Five Dynasties, Li Ye fixed a bamboo flute on the head of the paper eagle so that it would make music when the wind blew on it. Since then, kites have been known as *fengzheng* 风筝 (wind *zheng*, *zheng* being a traditional stringed instrument).

The kite expresses Mankind's ambition to take to the skies. It was the first flying contraption invented. The invention of the aeroplane had its inspiration from the humble kite. Many flying activities today also evolved from the kite.

Football

More than 3,000 years ago, the Chinese kicked a rock around as a football. During the Yin-Shang Dynasty, the people would pray for rain as they kicked and danced around with the football. The Warring States Period had a ball woven from fur. Later, a leather ball was filled with hair and fur. It was called *taju* 蹋鞠 and was used for recreational purposes.

During the Western Han Period, football became a form of military training.

Shuttlecock

The history of the shuttlecock probably goes back 2,000 years to the Han Dynasty. During the Tang Dynasty, the Shaolin monks in Henan were believed to have kicked the shuttlecock as part of their martial arts training. The imperial concubines also enjoyed this activity. Kicking the shuttlecock was one of the two favourite recreational activities in the palace, the other being the swing.

Swing

There are many stories of how the swing came about. The earliest version has it that the swing was used by the ancient people in the western region for military training. During the Spring and Autumn Period, to save the state of Yan, Ji Heng led an army and seized the swing. Over the years, the swing gradually grew in popularity. It is also said that the swing was invented during the Han Dynasty to celebrate Emperor Hanwu's 1,000th birthday. It was originally called *qianqiu* 千秋 (1,000 autumns).

Bamboo tube

Made from a type of bamboo, the two ends of the bamboo tube had two round boxes. The small holes in the round boxes would make sounds as the bamboo was twirled. The more holes there were, the louder the sound. As one twirls the bamboo tube, one's hands may take on different positions to create a myriad of patterns. You may not know this, but the yo-yo that we play with today has its origins in the bamboo tube.

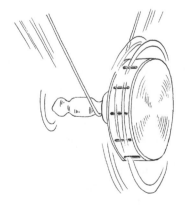

Spinning top

The spinning top is similar to the single bamboo tube. But it is played on the ground instead. Some tops could produce a sound as they were spun. These were also known as ground cows. People in northeastern China call the top Ice Monkey as children play the game during winter. As the top spins on a thick layer of ice, it looks as lively as a monkey.

Chinese rings

Chinese rings are metal strips that have been twisted into interesting shapes. They are intertwined and the aim is to separate the intertwined pieces through a set sequence of moves. After this is accomplished, the player can also try to join the pieces back together. Chinese rings come in various configurations: five-piece, seven-piece, nine-piece, 11-piece, 13-piece and so forth, with the most popular being the nine-piece configuration.

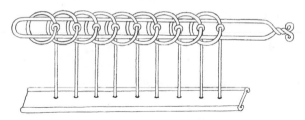

Seven-part puzzle

This is an ancient type of jigsaw puzzle, in the shape of a square, which has been divided into various shapes. It can be rearranged in many different ways. The seven-part puzzle originated from the *yanji* 燕几 a table invented during the Tang Dynasty for use at banquets. The *yanji* could be extended or dismantled according to the number of guests at the banquet. It was also called the seven-star table. Later, the table inspired the development of thin wooden pieces or thick paper to create a jigsaw puzzle game, which then became known as the seven-part puzzle.

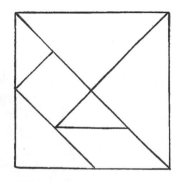

Martial Arts

Chinese martial arts draws from ancient Chinese philosophy and aesthetics, emphasising oneness between heaven and Man (*tian ren he yi* 天人合一), and beauty in form and spirit (*xing shen jian mei* 形神兼美). The student of martial arts must be in harmony with the changes of Heaven and Earth, and not only must the form be pleasing, one must also cultivate the inner essence (*jing* 精), vital energy (*qi* 气) and spirit (*shen* 神), to truly master Chinese martial arts.

The different schools

Among the many schools of Chinese martial arts, the most famous are Shaolin and Wudang.

Shaolin *gongfu* has an external focus, characterised by aggressive moves and swift counterattack. Tradition holds that 'all Chinese martial arts stem from Shaolin'. It is said to have been founded by an Indian monk, Bodhidharma, in 520 AD. Shaolin Monastery, located in China's He'nan Province, is a mecca for martial-arts lovers worldwide.

Wudang *gongfu*, on the other hand, stresses internal strength; its moves are gentle, and use inertia to conquer movement. Legend has it that the Wudang Sect was founded during the Ming Dynasty, by a Taoist priest named Zhang Sanfeng 张三丰.

Boxing arts

There are numerous schools of Chinese boxing (unarmed combat). Some are named after founding familes, such as the Chen-, Yang- and Wu-style *taiji* boxing. Others are named after the regions from which they originated, such as Shaolin and Emei Boxing. The rest are named after animals, such as the Mantis and Monkey styles, and so on.

Weapon arts

Weapon arts refer to the use of weaponry (arms) in martial arts. There are many types of weapons, and they can be divided largely into long weapons (spear, cudgel, pike, etc), short weapons (sabre, sword, etc), soft weapons (nine-section whip, three-section cudgel, etc) and hidden weapons. Out of the entire arms selection, the sabre and sword are the most popular. These two types of weapons are often paired up in mention, for instance: "The sabre is like a ferocious tiger, the sword like a gliding dragon".

Martial ethics

The world of martial arts strongly emphasises martial ethics or chivalry (*wude* 武德). Adages on the subject include 'Heavier than mountains is chivalry; lighter than grass are fame and fortune'; 'Virtue is first in martial arts', 'First master the code of ethics', etc. This is because martial arts gives its practitioners an edge over other people. A virtuous pugilist could benefit his fellow men, but an unscrupulous one could turn out to be a scourge of the people.

Directory of Food and Retail Outlets

SINGAPORE'S CHINESE RESTAURANTS

Dragon Pearl Restaurant
#05-09 Ngee Ann City
391 Orchard Road
Singapore 238872
Tel: 6737 1788 Fax: 6834 0178
Website: www.dragonpearl.com

Tian Jin House of Delicacies
80 Pagoda Street
Singapore 059239
Tel: 6323 5885

Chinatown Food Street
Along Smith Street in Chinatown, you can taste Teochew, Hokkien, Hainanese and Hakka culinary delights.

Da Dong Restaurant
39 Smith Street
Singapore 058952 Tel: 6221 3906
Holds an "opera lunch session" from 10am to 3pm every Saturday.

Yan Palace Restaurant
Blk 531 Upper Cross Street
#04-38 Hong Lim Complex
Singapore 050531
Tel: 6222 2516 Fax: 6533 2013

Dragon City Sichuan Restaurant
Copthorne Orchid (Plymouth Wing)
214 Dunearn Road
Singapore 299526
Tel: 6254 7070 Fax: 6255 6390

TEA HOUSES & THE TEA TRADE

Tea Chapter Trading
No 9A, 11, 11A Neil Road
Singapore 088808
Tel: 6226 1175 Fax: 6221 0604

TenRen's Tea
259 South Bridge Road
Singapore 058808
Tel: 6423 9433 Fax: 6735 8254

D'ART STATION
No. 65 Pagoda Street
Singapore 059224
Tel: 6225 8307

LEARNING THE ARTS

Singapore Xiangqi General Association
51 Bishan Street 13
#01-01 Singapore 579799
Tel: 6259 0984 Fax: 6258 8125

Imperial Herbal Restaurant
3rd Floor Metropole Hotel
41 Seah Street
Singapore 188396
Tel: 6337 0491

CHINESE MEDICINE HALLS

Eu Yan Sang
269A South Bridge Road
Singapore 058818
Tel: 6223 6333 Fax: 6324 6789
Website: www.euyansang.com

Thye Shan Medical Hall
201 New Bridge Road
Singapore 059428
Tel: 6223 1326 Fax: 6221 5042

HST Medical Pte Ltd
101 Upper Cross Street
#05-34 People's Park Centre
Singapore 058357
Tel: 6536 5108
Website: www.heritage.com.sg

Singapore Calligraphy Centre
48 Waterloo Street Singapore 187952
Tel: 6337 7753

Singapore Weiqi Association
116 Middle Road
#03-04 ICE Enterprise House
Singapore 188972
Tel: 6339 7726 Fax: 6334 3580
51 Bishan Street 13
#02-01 Singapore 579799
Tel: 6356 9756 Fax: 6353 3105
Website: www.weiqi.org.sg

Chinese Theatre Circle
No.5A Smith Street
Singapore 058919
Tel: 6323 4862 Fax: 6324 1681
*Chinese opera seminars and demonstrations
held every Friday and Saturday from
7pm – 9pm.*

Singapore National Wushu Federation
50 Serangoon Avenue 2
#04-01 Singapore 556129
Tel: 6746 3026

Hsinghai Art Association
155 Waterloo Street
#01-11 Stamford Arts Centre
Singapore 187962
Tel: 6339 5405
Chinese music courses.

Community Centre/Clubs
Website: www.pa.gov.sg
*Most community clubs offer short
courses on playing the* erhu *and*
guzheng *or practising* taiji *or wushu.*

HANDICRAFTS

Yue Hwa Chinese Products
70 Eu Tong Sen Street
Singapore 6538 4222
Tel: 6538 4222 Fax: 6538 4233
Handicrafts, costumes and medicine.

BAO YUAN TRADING PTE LTD
15,17 #01-03 Temple Street
Singapore 058562
Tel: 6227 1189 Fax: 6227 2139

S.I. WOOD CARVER
35 Pagoda Street Singapore 059194
Tel: 6323 3371 Fax: 6323 1227

YONG GALLERY
260 South Bridge Road
Singapore 058809
Tel/Fax: 6226 1718
*Chinese handicrafts; seal carving and
Chinese calligraphy demonstrations.*

CHIN HING EMPORIUM
55 Pagoda Street
Singapore 059214
Tel: 6323 1210
*Qipaos, Tang costumes and
Chinese-style children's clothing.*

*There are many shops selling handicrafts along Pagoda Street, Temple Street and
Smith Street. Qipaos or Tang costumes may also be purchased or custom-made.*

MUSEUMS AND OTHERS

Asian Civilisations Museum
39 Armenian Street
Singapore 179941
Tel: 6332 3284 Fax: 6883 0732
Website: www.nhb.gov.sg/ACM/acm.shtml

**SINGAPORE FEDERATION OF
CHINESE CLAN ASSOCIATIONS**
397 Lorong 2 Toa Payoh
Singapore 319639
Tel: 6337 3965

Chinatown Heritage Centre
48 Pagoda Street
Singapore 059207
Tel: 6325 2878 Fax: 6325 2879
Website:
www.chinatownheritage.com.sg

The Directory is intended to be a resource for anyone who wants to initiate contact
with individuals, companies and organisations with Chinese-related concerns. If you
run a relevant business or workshop, send us your particulars via email:
asiapacbooks@pacific.net.sg or fax: (65) 6392 6455. Listing is free.

Map of Chinatown

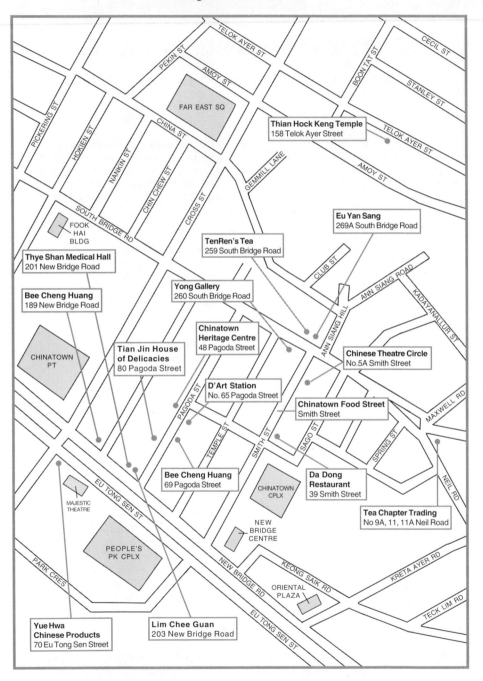

Glossary of Common Phrases

English	Chinese
Good morning.	早安。（zǎo-ān）
Good afternoon.	午安。（wǔ-ān）
Good evening.	晚安。（wǎn-ān）
How are you?	你好吗？（nǐ hǎo ma）
I am fine.	很好。（hěn hǎo）
My name is …	我的名字是……（wǒ de míng·zi shì…）
Thank you.	谢谢。（xièxie）
Don't mention it.	不客气。（búkèqi）
I am sorry.	对不起。（duìbuqǐ）
I don't understand.	我不明白。（wǒ bù míngbai）
Happy Birthday!	生日快乐！（shēngri kuàilè）
See you again / goodbye.	再见。（zàijiàn）

Do's and Don'ts in Chinese Culture

Birthdays
- We may give red packets or other gifts like toys or baby necessities when we attend a baby's one-month-old celebration.
- Be dressed appropriately while attending an elderly person's birthday celebration. Avoid wearing black or white. Birthday gifts may come in the form of red packets, tonics, tonic wines and the like.
- Do avoid giving anyone a clock (*song zhong*) as it rhymes with burying a parent (*song zhong*). It is considered inauspicious.

Weddings
- The amount of money in the red packet that you give to the bridal couple must be an even number. Write your name on the back of the red packet.
- The host will usually have the seating arrangements planned beforehand. Do not sit at any table you like.
- Chinese wedding dinners are usually a long affair. Try to avoid leaving halfway through the dinner. At the end of the dinner, the bridal couple and the hosts will thank and bid guests farewell at the entrance.
- Whether it is a birthday, wedding or another happy occasion, it is polite to prepare a gift or red packet for the host. You may also ask another person to deliver the gift on your behalf. It is a way to congratulate the host.

In general, you may give red packets for happy occasions. But red packets come in a myriad of designs. So make sure you select the appropriate one.

Funerals
- Dress in sombre colours and appropriate attire when attending a funeral wake.
- There are no rules about the amount of money gifted to the bereaved family. It is not necessary to place the money in an envelope. You may also give a flower wreath.
- Offer incense and bow to the deceased three times as a show of respect when you arrive at the funeral wake.

- It is not necessary to bid the bereaved family goodbye when you leave the funeral wake.

The Chinese have many taboos where death is concerned. You should avoid attending a funeral and a wedding on the same day. Also, avoid going to another person's house after going to a funeral wake.

What a guest should do
- Unless the host has invited you over for a meal, try not to time your visit at mealtimes. You should also inform the host beforehand about your visit.
- You may bring gifts like cakes and snacks when you visit someone. The host will usually try to decline the gift before accepting it. The Chinese do not usually open the gifts in front of the guest as they deem it rude.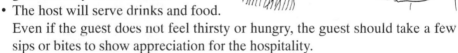
- The host will serve drinks and food. Even if the guest does not feel thirsty or hungry, the guest should take a few sips or bites to show appreciation for the hospitality.
- The guest should take the initiative to end the visit and thank the host for the hospitality. The host will usually ask the guest to stay longer as a courtesy.

Meeting for the first time
- Nowadays, when meeting someone for the first time, the Chinese will offer a handshake. If one is wearing gloves, the gloves should be removed first. Generally, the lady will offer her hand first in a handshake exchange between a man and a woman. She may also just nod her head and smile instead.
- During the Lunar New Year or other happy occasions, you may clasp your hands before your chest to congratulate the host or the other party.
- When you meet an elderly person, you may bow slightly to show respect.
- When you are walking with elders or guests, do not walk ahead of them. Move to the side at the entrance to a building or place. Let them go in first.

HISTORY EXPRESS

HISTORY EXPRESS chronicles world cultures and the prominent individuals and events that have influenced the story of mankind. The series offers quick access to important historical events and personalities.

We have launched this series with the history of China.

Relive 5,000 years of Chinese civilization in comics:
- Chinese History
- Great Chinese Emperors
- Infamous Chinese Emperors
- Chinese Imperial Women
- Secrets of the Chinese Palace
- Famous Chinese Diplomats
- The Great Sage Confucius
- The Great Explorer Cheng Ho

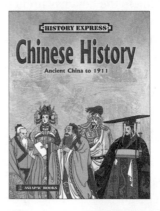

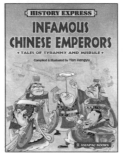

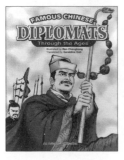

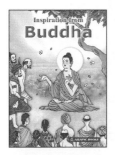

INSPIRATION FROM BUDDHA

Through skilful means, Buddha taught kings and commoners how living a life of morality, compassion and wisdom could bring the meaning to existence. This engagingly illustrated book of Buddha's teachings is relevant and appealing to readers young and old alike.
Illustrated by **Fu Chunjiang**. *208pp, 150x210mm, ISBN 978-981-229-511-8*

ZEN INSPIRATION

Zen is a way of creative living. In this book, you will find out about Zen in all its vitality and simplicity. Whatever it is about Zen that fascinates you – silent meditation or creative expression – you will not be disappointed as you dip into the pages of this book.
Illustrated by **Fu Chunjiang**. *224pp, 150x210mm, ISBN 981-229-455-4.*

THE TAO INSPIRATION :
Essence of Lao Zi's Wisdom

Written more than 2,500 years ago, the Tao Te Ching now comes in 21st century style. Presenting Lao Zi's masterpiece in a concise, comprehensive yet profound manner, this book provides practical wisdom for leadership and for achieving balance and harmony in everyday life.
Illustrated by **Feng Ge**. *176pp, 150x210mm, ISBN 981-229-396-5.*

INSPIRATION FROM CONFUCIUS:
Choice Quotations from the Analects

More than 100 choice quotations classified under broad themes depicting Confucian core values and enhanced by inspirational thoughts. With additional features on Confucius' life, achievements and influence, it makes an excellent representation of the *Analects*.
Illustrated by **Jeffrey Seow**. *224pp, 150x210mm, ISBN 981-229-398-1.*

中华文化之旅

绘画 ：傅春江

翻译 ：韩玉与谢美芳

亚太图书有限公司出版